SYNTHESIZING GRAVITY

SYNTHESIZING GRAVITY

Selected Prose

KAY RYAN

WINNER OF THE PULITZER PRIZE

Edited and with an Introduction
by Christian Wiman

Grove Press
New York

FIRST EDITION

Published simultaneously in Canada
Printed in the United States of America

First Grove Atlantic hardcover edition: April 2020

This book is set in 12-point Bembo
by Alpha Design & Composition of Pittsfield, NH

Library of Congress Cataloging-in-Publication data
is available for this title.

ISBN 978-0-8021-4818-6
eISBN 978-0-8021-4819-3

Grove Press
an imprint of Grove Atlantic
154 West 14th Street
New York, NY 10011

Distributed by Publishers Group West

groveatlantic.com

20 21 22 23 24   10 9 8 7 6 5 4 3 2 1

Credits

The following pieces first appeared in these publications:

"A Consideration of Poetry" originally appeared in *Poetry,* May 2006

"Derichment" originally appeared in *The Ruminator Review,* Summer 2000

"I go to AWP" originally appeared in *Poetry,* July/August 2005

"Specks" originally appeared in *Poetry,* September 2013

"Notes on the Danger of Notebooks" originally appeared as "Notes on the Danger of Keeping Notebooks" in *Parnassus: Poetry In Review,* Vol. 23, nos. 1 & 2, 1998

"Do You Like It?" originally appeared in *ZYZZYVA,* Winter 1998

"The Authority of Lightness," a review of *Stevie: A Biography of Stevie Smith,* by Jack Barbera and William McBrien, originally appeared in *The Threepenny Review,* Winter 1990

"Inedible Melons," a review of *The Poems of Marianne Moore*, ed. Grace Schulman, originally appeared in *Yale Review*, Spring 2004

"Fidget and Gnash," a review of *The Selected Letters of Marianne Moore*, ed. Bonnie Costello, originally appeared in *Boston Review*, Summer 1998

"I Demand to Speak With God," a review of *The Notebooks of Robert Frost*, ed. Robert Faggen, originally appeared in *Poetry*, September 2007

"Wang-Pang-Woo-Poo-Woof-Woof," a review of *Letters of Wallace Stevens*, ed. Holly Stevens, originally appeared in *Boston Review*, Summer 1997

"The Trail of the Hunted Wolf," a review of *Conversations with Joseph Brodsky: A Poet's Journey Through the Twentieth Century*, by Solomon Volkov, translated by Marian Schwarz, originally appeared in *The Hungry Mind Review*, Fall 1998

"Only Doubts," a review of *This Craft of Verse* by Jorge Luis Borges, originally appeared as "Profound Lightness" in *The Threepenny Review*, Winter 2003

"Flying," a review of *An American Childhood* by Annie Dillard originally appeared in *The Threepenny Review*, Summer 1988

"The Abrasion of Loneliness" is from the author's personal archive

"On a Poem by Hopkins" is from the author's personal archive

"Radiantly Indefensible" is from the author's personal archive

"All Love All Beauty" is from the author's personal archive

"On a Poem by Dickinson" is from the author's personal archive

"No Time for Anything but Repetition" is from the author's personal archive

"The End of the Party" is from the author's personal archive

"All the Nothing" is from the author's personal archive

"Listening to Williams," written in response to an archival recording of William Carlos Williams's 1954 reading at the Unterberg Poetry Center of the 92nd St. Y, was originally published online as part of the Center's *75 at 75* anniversary celebration, 2013

"Con and Pro," originally published as "Antagonism: Walt Whitman" in *Poetry*, October 2004 and as "Enthusiasm: William Bronk" in *Poetry*, March 2006

"The Double" originally appeared in *Poetry*, April 2005

"Reading Before Breakfast" originally appeared in *The Hungry Mind Review*, Summer 1998

"To Be Miniature Is to Be Swallowed by a Miniature Whale," written as part of a symposium on The Miniature, originally published in *The Threepenny Review*, Spring 2016

"Against Influence," originally published as "Essay on Influence," was written for the Centennial celebration of the Pulitzer Prizes and originally published online at pulitzer.org, February 2016

"On Forgetting" was originally published as "Memory and Forgetting" in *Speakeasy*, Fall 2005

"The Edges of Time," written as an introduction to the poem "The Edges of Time," originally published in "Poet's Choice" column, *The Washington Post*, September 25, 2009

"The Poet Takes a Walk" originally published as "Marin County, Sort Of" as a "The Poet Takes a Walk" feature in *Poetry*, November 2009

"My House" was originally published in *Freeman's: Home*, April 2017

For Carol

Contents

III

IV

Introduction

In C. S. Lewis's *The Great Divorce* a few souls travel from hell (on a bus, naturally) to heaven only to discover that everything is too heavy for them. Water is rock and apples are iron. A mere leaf is, for the unenlightened, unbudgeable. The book makes you crave the reality of this new world (which is the old world, naturally), makes you want to be one of the souls who can drink from its streams and savor its tastes. Kay Ryan is not religious, but I can't help thinking that she and Lewis are in some way native to the same imagined place, a realm in which gravity and levity are vivid kin:

> Right now I am thinking of something unlikely that I saw a few days ago, the morning after my town had experienced a major winter flood. In the middle of a residential street, a cast-iron manhole cover was dancing in its collar, driven up three or four inches by such an excess of underground water that it balanced above the street, tipping and

bobbing like a flower, occasionally producing a bell-like chime as it touched against the metal ring. This has much to say about poetry.

That's from the first page of "A Consideration of Poetry," the first essay in this volume, and it has "much to say" about all that follows. From that miraculous manhole cover at the outset, to the tour of the house that is a tour of the mind at the end, this book achieves a kind of "sustained impossibility," to use a phrase that Ryan herself uses to describe the work of Marianne Moore. Ryan has a way of tweezering immensities, so that you can see, as in a three-dimensional diagram, entire bodies of work before the mind's eye. She is bristly and funny and contradictory: against notebooks, against influence, against glut, and then—suddenly, savingly—against being against: "*If we are not compelled to submit in some way to a poem it cannot change us.*" The economy of the book belies its range. Aside from the criticism, there are quick hits on memory and forgetting, the audience for poetry, the miniature in art. There is a freestanding and freewheeling piece in which she goes, like Samuel Johnson on safari, to the largest writers' conference in the country. There's even a conversion (to poetry, naturally). A few of these essays have never been seen before and arrived at my door in pencil, each without a word crossed out and bearing such boreal clarity and crisp precisions that I found myself pausing to write things down. One could make a large commonplace book out of this small collection of uncommon essays:

> Embarrassment at being human may be a deeper provocation to artistic production than we usually think.

> When Gertrude Stein was at last after so many years of fruitful absence touring and lecturing in the United States, she was a popular sensation in that she was of a piece, a figure round and burrless as a ball, solid, simple, capable of being perfectly, not partially, misunderstood.

> It's the strangest thing; the poem is a trap—that is a release. It's a small door to a room full of gold that we can have any time we go through the door, but that we can't *take away*."

> There must be a crack in the poet of some sort. It has to be deep, privately potent, and unmendable— and the poet must forever try to mend it.

> There is something repellent in all this. But I am convinced that for a poet to be great we must find ourselves repelled by some part of the poet's work.

There is a permanent time that poetry lets us into.
There are doors in all the centuries, feeding into
this permanent time.

She could get high C out of a potato.

Notice the metaphors. They crackle through prac-
tically every paragraph. Indeed Ryan's mind adverts
to metaphor so readily some might think it a tic. But
metaphor is where the creative imagination reveals its
furthest capacities. And its kinship with what is beyond
its capacities. This is a spiritual assertion, though to
understand it fully one might have to resist that adjec-
tive. "It is an elegant paradox that close application to
the physical somehow does release the mind from the
physical," Ryan writes of Moore. And of Stevie Smith:
"The most beautiful thoughts and feelings can barely
settle or they break us. We can't endure more than the
briefest visitations. That's the cruel fact. Almost every
writer almost always crushes her own work under the
weight of thoughts and feelings."

But "thoughts and feelings" are the whole point of
poetry in the end, as Ryan well knows. She emphasizes
the reserve of poetry so often, the "chillifier" of form that
emotion must go through to become art, that you might

not notice when the first few drips of real feeling infuse into the blood—then suddenly it's everywhere. Similarly, she is so insistently diminutive that you're shocked to find the cosmos crammed through the eye of a needle. ("One reason we're so fascinated by the tiniest pinholes is that we know we're going to have to go through the tiniest pinhole.") Her amiable porcupine pose is not a pose, exactly, but an adaptive technique. She is gregarious but allergic to agreement, in love with form but contemptuous of systems, acidically skeptical but as devoted to her own intuition as any mystic. "I will go so far as to hazard that blundering might be *generative*," she says in a discussion of a little-known poem by Emily Dickinson, "meaning that rooting around in a haystack long and fruitlessly enough could conceivably *breed a needle*." Do I need to point out the genius of "breed" here? That a certain amount of blundering about in an uneven but (now) unforgettable poem has bred a genuine insight, the pith and proof of which is sound itself? Probably not. One of the great charms of Ryan's mind is that she assumes her readers will keep up with her.

Speed is in fact a word she returns to when describing what she most values in poetry. It is important to understand what she means by this. It is not mere "quickness" or wit, and it has nothing to do with the surface associativeness that characterizes much contemporary poetry. There is nothing *nervous* about it. "We must be less in love with foreground if we want to see far," she writes, and that's the chief sensation I get from her thinking: vast distances covered with great speed. In her own poems, actually, this action isn't so much velocity as simultaneity, a kind of quantum thought. Images and ideas seem less sequential than instantaneous, as if reality were neural. Prose obeys different laws, though there are many passages in this book that will make you wonder just how clearly that line can be drawn.

The subjects of Ryan's critical attention are for the most part unsurprising. She might pause to swat the blob of Walt Whitman, and her takes on Annie Dillard and Marilynne Robinson (this one was in pencil) are bracing. Mostly, though, her critical gaze is like her poetic one: fixed and distant. She looks at poets who are like her in some way, and she looks, ever so lightly, *hard*. This kind of sympathetic criticism turns out to be a much more difficult enterprise than if she were surveying a wide range of writers. In that instance, one might appreciate (or not) her *taste*. But when like turns to like, and when the subjects are already so barnacled with laurels, the expectations become much greater. She'd better say something truly original about Marianne Moore, because otherwise what's the point. So she does: "It takes a deep security to endure a life of such endless lightness, tangled delicacy, nearly mad fealty to serial perfections, almost comic probity." One could memorize that line and be fortified against despair. And this miraculous essay ends: "Hers is a genius so perfectly self-tuned that we find ourselves laughing, one of the body's natural responses to shock."

That sentence is itself so perfectly self-tuned that I hesitate to point it out. It is a truism to say that a poet's criticism is always implicitly defensive, one part microscope and one part mirror. In fact it is true, or at least meaningful, only of great poets, whose mirrors *matter*. Of *course* one could say that Ryan's poems, along with Moore's, cheer and chill in equal measure. They do not ask you to love them. They do not want to "change your life." It is possible that you will love them and they will change your life, but that is on the other side of their primary purpose. What is that purpose, in Ryan's case? I would say it is to light the space between mind and world. To light, and thereby lighten, the space between mind and world. To lighten, and thereby *lessen*, the space between mind and world.

This ambition, which of course is not an "ambition" but a genetic gift and/or glitch, a compulsion of the blood, informs everything she says in the prose, though the thinking is so sprightly that it's easy to miss the canyons she's ambling over, cartoonlike, by not looking down. When she says, in a piece about taking a walk, that she has an odd but prodigious gift for matching distant bits of trash along the road, we hardly notice the immense intellectual and even metaphysical dimensions of this perception, even though she makes it for us: "The brain anticipates significance; it doesn't know which edge may in fifty yards knit to which other edge, so everything is held, charged with a subliminal glitter along its raw sides."

Subliminal glitter. That's more than a great phrase. If the shards of the world (and our experience) are charged with a subliminal glitter, if mind and matter seem to communicate with each other, seem so atomically entwined that the one might *breed a needle* in the other, then what does this say about our relationship to the world? Might that crack that runs through the consciousness of the poet, which is what drives one to write in the first place, and the unity of all creation, which every poem both intuits and pursues, be one day reconciled? Maybe reality really *is* neural? On the other hand, why muse on such mysteries when your brain can activate the thing itself? You might as well drop these imponderables on Ariel.

The mind (and its chief system, language) is Ryan's "flood subject," just as Emily Dickinson's was immortality and Stevie Smith's was, as Ryan tells us, "the cheering thought of suicide." I write that sentence and feel it to be true—yet I pause. If the mind is Ryan's flood subject, and if the mind's relation to the world is as I have sketched it, then there is an implicit rift under the flood. ("There must be a crack in the poet of some sort. . . .") The rift is loneliness. It's so narrow you often miss it under the levity and dexterity, and yet so deep that, just as with Dickinson (though hers isn't hidden), it can make sustained exposure to the work difficult and not at all without risk. I want to be very precise here. This is not the sort of loneliness a biography will ever explain, the sort that is defined by relationships and time. That kind of loneliness is, even if it is not answered, answerable. When Ryan writes (of Wallace Stevens) that "loneliness is not the grief for poets that it is for others," it's this kind of loneliness she's talking about. But the polar note in her own poems is closer to Lear's lonely "nevers" (one of her most devastating poems is called "The First of Never") and is indeed the grief for poets that it is for others. This note is not at all prominent in Ryan's work, is in fact often barely perceptible, but it underlies her entire vision, and without it the poems would not have the glinting depths they do.

Ideal Audience

Not scattered legions,
not a dozen from
a single region
for whom accent
matters, not a seven-
member coven,
not five shirttail
cousins; just
one free citizen—
maybe not alive
now even—who
will know with
exquisite gloom
that only we two
ever found this room.

I can't tell you how much pure elation this gives me. I included it in an anthology called *Joy*, though in the end I think it's a poem of almost irremediable loneliness. *Almost* irremediable. The connections one makes through poetry are not complete, but there is joy in that. Perhaps I should say *and* there is joy in that, because one of the things that art teaches is that we are connected in ways at once too deep to reach in any other way, and yet beyond the reach of art. This is, for some poets, so much a matter of sound. The music of Gerard Manley Hopkins's "Spring and Fall," which Ryan says is an utterly anti-Christian poem, seems to me to offer a solace that is more powerful (and certainly more *durable*) than any sermon I have heard. Ryan is exquisitely attentive to this solace, because she is exquisitely attentive to sound. For all her insistence on lightness, deftness, the "dissolution of weight," she knows that great art demands a release into all that you do not understand but understand your very survival depends upon. She also knows the necessary deformities that great poetry emerges from, temporarily ameliorates, and, alas, exacerbates. "We truly see that the difficult Wallace Stevens we sense from the poems was not a pose or a reduction but a very brave and unrelenting articulation of his own impossibility."

Impossibility. There's that word again. The manhole cover still bobbing and belling above the flood.

What a triumph this book is, partly because it is more than a book. Ryan has forged—no other verb will do, for it has taken great patience and will—a style of art that is also a style of life. Such strong economy comes with limitations, of course, but the compensations are immense. It is a style capable of withstanding great pressure. It repels all manner of cant, gush, and less-than-exquisite gloom. Sometimes just a drop of it serves as a kind of existential smelling salts: "She gives us poems in shapes that might result in a chamber free of the heart's gravity." It's not a fashionable notion. That limits liberate, that there can be in some forms of refusal the greatest freedom (another crucial word for Ryan's aesthetic), that all life's troubles and treasures might be—I think of Julian of Norwich suddenly seeing all of creation in a single hazelnut—a matter of syntax. Again and again you think to yourself: this lightness can't be all there is. And it isn't. It's more that "all there is" is, for a moment, lightness. "Give me a lever and I could move the universe," said Archimedes. Keen readers have known for years that Ryan's poems are such levers. Now the world will learn it of her prose.

Christian Wiman

I

A Consideration of Poetry

I: POETRY IS FUNNY

I have always felt that much of the best poetry was funny. Who can read Hopkins's "The Windhover," for instance, and not feel welling up inside a kind of giddiness indistinguishable from the impulse to laugh? I suppose there has got to be some line where one might say about a poem, "That's *too much* nonsense," but I think it is a line worth tempting. I am sure that there is a giggly aquifer under poetry, it so often makes me want to laugh.

Right now I am thinking of something unlikely that I saw a few days ago, the morning after my town had experienced a major winter flood. In the middle of a residential street, a cast-iron manhole cover was dancing in its iron collar, driven up three or four inches by such an excess of underground water that it balanced above the street, tipping and bobbing like a flower, occasionally producing a bell-like chime as it touched against the metal ring. This has much to say about poetry.

For I do not want to suggest in any way that this aquifer under poetry is something silly or undangerous; it is great and a causer of every sort of damage. And I do not want to say either that the poem that prompts me to laughter is silly or light; no, it can be as heavy as a manhole cover, but it is forced up. You can see it would take an exquisite set of circumstances to ever get this right.

I would like to offer as an illustration a poem that has always elicited from me one of those involuntary *ha!*s that jump out when you've witnessed a wonderful magic trick. You might say that isn't funny; you might say you'd just been punched in a way that had exacted a *ha!* Maybe that *ha!* is the body's natural response to perfection: a perfect trick (one has been utterly deceived) or a perfect poem (one has been utterly deceived).

In any case, here is the poem, Robert Frost's "Nothing Gold Can Stay":

> Nature's first green is gold,
> Her hardest hue to hold.
> Her early leaf's a flower;
> But only so an hour.

Then leaf subsides to leaf.
So Eden sank to grief,
So dawn goes down to day.
Nothing gold can stay.

Where is the laughter? you ask. Well, don't ask yet. For now please settle for a more generalized sense of amusement, of the high-toned T. S. Eliot variety (*The Sacred Wood*):

> Poetry is a superior amusement. I do not mean an amusement for superior people. I call it an amusement, an amusement *pour distraire les honnêtes gens*, not because that is a true definition, but because if you call it anything else you are likely to call it something still more false. If we think of the nature of amusement, then poetry is not amusing; but if we think of anything else that poetry may seem to be, we are led into far greater difficulties.

I love two things about Eliot's definition. First, the bedrock, indefensible truth of it: that poetry is a superior amusement. Second, Eliot's mess of an attempt to explain what he means. I am heartened in my own efforts when I see his bluster. I am reminded by him that though we cannot be exactly precise or complete, that is no reason not to make gigantic statements, for there is great enjoyment in gigantic statements.

But to return to Frost's poem. I have chosen it because it's about as funny as the Farmer's Almanac. Had I chosen "The Windhover," there would be the obvious near gibberish that comes from Hopkins's supersaturated rhyming and his strange bulging liberties with sense, but Frost's poem couldn't be less gibberishy or less apparently nonsensical.

What could be more straightforward? The title is repeated as the last line—as though this little stack of an eight-line poem were a bitter sandwich with a filling compounded of evidence that nothing gold can stay. The gold that precedes green in new plants? Pfft! The way little new leaf clusters on trees look like flowers? Again, pfft! And notice that by the second couplet we have already moved away from the literal "gold" that exists briefly before the "first green" and are beginning our relentless slide into metaphorical gold—in the sense of something precious—with the flower's superiority to the later leaf. Now things speed up geometrically, as "leaf *subsides* to leaf." There is no doubt of Frost's

meaning here: the early, the delicate, the golden—all go down, buried under the grosser, heartier, darker, more leathery giant repulsive leaves of maturity and stink.

But that's just in the natural world; how about humankind? Another pfft!: "So Eden sank to grief"— another ring of maturity and stink. Look at how Frost intensifies the sensation of falling (or being overcome) with his choice of verbs: first that unnerving "subsides" among the leaves, now full-out "sank" for man: something is always pulling the plug and draining the gold.

Well, so it goes for nature, and for humanity, but there's still the planet; how about it? Pfft!: "So dawn *goes down* to day." It is odd, this thought of dawn (a kind of gold) defeated by day. We usually say, "day breaks," or "the sun comes up," something to suggest a beginning, an opening, a rising and spreading. Not here; here day is a corrupter, a violence that drives dawn down. No trick in this poem: nothing gold can stay.

Except wait a minute! Has gold ever been more manifest than in this poem? Nothing makes us treasure something like feeling we're right then losing it. This poem is *all* trick; Frost spreads before us (like a magician's deck) the gold of the first green, the early flower,

Eden, and dawn, one after another, snatches them away, and still the gold remains; it's suspended within the poem shivering between being and being palmed.

And that's poetry, this impossible pang, which seen another way is a tremendous bullying job to which we submitted before we knew it. We're done for so fast we can't stop to think, "Who SAYS leaf *subsides*—rather than *advances*—to leaf, or that dawn *goes down*—rather than *expands*—to day?" Too late; we're stuck in Frost's little house, shingled in with the overlapping arguments; nailed down with the tidy rhymed couplets. It's the strangest thing; the poem is a trap—that is a release. It's a small door to a room full of gold that we can have any time we go through the door, but that we can't *take away*.

Ha!

At about nine months, a baby starts to laugh when something is suddenly taken away from her. One of a baby's first games is peek-a-boo, where someone repeatedly disappears and reappears (the enjoyment of which is, incidentally, considered a key indicator of later language acquisition skills). Frost's poem could be thought of as a kind of peek-a-boo. The rhythm of its repeated take-aways may go all the way back to our deep early enjoyment of loss, which we register with laughter.

If this strikes you as nonsense, it is. Something non-sensical in the heart of poetry is the very reason why one can't call poetry "useful." Sense is useful; you can apply things that make sense to other circumstances; you can take something away. But nonsense you can only revisit; its satisfactions exist in it, and not in applications. This is why Auden and others can say with such confidence that poetry makes nothing happen. That's the relief of it. And the reason why nothing can substitute for it.

II: GOSKY PATTIES

Now would be a good time to think more about the elements of nonsense when it sails under its own colors. And where better to look for them than in a small nonsense recipe by Edward Lear:

TO MAKE GOSKY PATTIES

Take a Pig, three or four years of age, and tie him by the off-hind leg to a post. Place 5 pounds of currants, 3 of sugar, 2 pecks of peas, 18 roast chestnuts, a candle, and six bushels of turnips, within his reach; if he eats these, constantly provide him with more.

Then procure some cream, some slices of Cheshire cheese, four quires of foolscap paper, and a packet of black pins. Work the whole into a paste, and spread it out to dry on a sheet of clean brown water-proof linen.

When the paste is perfectly dry, but not before, proceed to beat the Pig violently, with the handle of a large broom. If he squeals, beat him again.

Visit the paste and beat the Pig alternately for some days, and ascertain if at the end of that period the whole is about to turn into Gosky Patties.

If it does not then, it never will; and in that case the Pig may be let loose, and the whole process may be considered as finished.

—*The Complete Nonsense of Edward Lear*
(Dover, 1951)

Many of the nonsense elements that animate Gosky Patties animate poetry as well:

1. AN INVENTED GOAL. Nobody, previously, wanted Gosky Patties made, just as no one wants a poem made. There is the occasional requirement of poets laureate to memorialize a bridge but that hardly counts. In general, one does not "find a need and fill it," as Henry Ford urged inventors to do. There is no need which precedes either nonsense or a poem. The creator is entertaining him or herself.

2. COWBIRD TECHNIQUE. Just as the cowbird lays her eggs in another bird's nest, nonsense is built inside the nest of some traditional form. It isn't just shapeless. Here, in "Gosky Patties," Lear takes over the recipe. Sometimes it's a botany or an alphabet. Or, on a smaller scale, a nonsense word may be fitted into the nest of perfectly good sense. Take "Gosky *Patties*" here, or, in "The Owl and the Pussycat," "runcible *spoons*." Nonsense's habit of taking up residence in something formal creates a feeling of order and propriety. Similarly, the poet occupies some sort of form. This may be the traditional form the poem takes, a sonnet or a villanelle, or simply a rhyme scheme. Or it may be a type of poem—say an epithalamium. Or it may be something else, perhaps a definition, or a list, or a claim to explain something. (I myself like to write "how-something-works" poems.) These things lend order and propriety. Form gives us confidence that we are not wasting our time on shapeless nonsense. (That's a joke of course; nonsense is *always* shaped. You can distinguish real nonsense from garbage because nonsense is shaped and tense.)

3. EXACTNESS. The nonsense writer is exact about things that only become important because he is exact

about them: "Take a Pig, *three or four years of age*, and tie him by *the off-hind* leg." There is little slop here. Similarly, the exactness of a poem's distinctions makes us feel that the distinctions matter. We suddenly care, for example, when Marianne Moore describes the shell of the paper nautilus in her poem by that name, with its "wasp-nest flaws / of white on white." We just feel that something precise is something important.

4. INCONGRUITY. Nonsense revels in working incompatible elements "*into a paste*." For example, "some cream, some slices of Cheshire cheese, four quires of foolscap paper, and a packet of black pins." The poet too feels that things which bear no outward relationship to one another must nonetheless be brought into proximity. Think of Marianne Moore's connection of "mussels" to "injured fans" in "The Fish." Or simply think of "injured fans"; that's great enough.

5. A SENSE OF IMMINENCE. Lear's instructions contain the faith that something is about to happen: "ascertain if . . . the whole is about to turn into Gosky Patties." Things are on the verge of coming together— which is more exciting than things having actually

come together, of course. A poem, for both the writer and reader, must have this same buildup, as to a sneeze. Nonsense is not directionless, any more than a poem is; both must have the feeling of going someplace. Nonsense, like poetry, is a kind of game, with rules or requirements. Neither is pointless, endless play, like that endless horsies whinnying and prancing thing girls do, or that strange martial arts sequence by which small boys advance through rooms. Play assumes that there is no end. Game (nonsense and poetry) assumes there is—if only for the sake of seeing it thwarted.

6. A HIGHLY PERSONAL IDEA OF CAUSE AND EFFECT. Lear insists that there *is* a relationship between the pig, the pig's placement, the pig's diet, the beating of the pig, and the paste, which may bring about Gosky Patties, although then again it may not. We must accept all this on faith for we know nothing about such things. We simply know that there *is* cause and effect in nonsense, as we know it in a poem—some interior machinery that must strike and tap and rotate in a particular sequence to get something to happen, beknownst only to the author. As readers, we like this. It's nice not to be in charge of cause and effect all the time, as we feel we are in "real life."

7. THE READER IS MADE INTO A CO-CONSPIRATOR.

This is in contradiction to the previous point, which is not a problem. We are treated both peremptorily and as equals. It is assumed—wrongly, of course—that the reader shares the knowledge of what Gosky Patties would be if they were to become themselves. There is this sense of *shared delicate sensibility* between reader and author about this: the reader must use *judgment* equal to the author's: "Visit the paste and beat the Pig alternately for some days, and ascertain if at the end of that period the whole is about to turn into Gosky Patties." You'll know what to do.

And so of course with poetry. We have the flattering feeling in reading a poem that we are somehow creating it. We're sending it where it goes. And in a way this is absolutely true, since the poem is only reconstituted by our act of reading and understanding, the letters otherwise quite helpless on the page. One might note, further, that in both the case of Lear's nonsense and in a poem, the thing that is being asked of us, such as knowing when Gosky Patties are about to form, may be pure hokum. We may understand it as hokum, and remain exactly as willing to get on with the show. Perhaps more willing, since who wants more practical outcomes.

8. A PERFECT ABSENCE OF SENTIMENT. The pig's feelings do not concern us. The pig is provided endless (primarily) tasty food (except the candle). The pig is at the same time beaten: ". . . beat the Pig violently, with the handle of a large broom. . . . Visit the paste and beat the Pig alternately for some days." If the whole doesn't turn into Gosky Patties, "the Pig may be let loose." (We may ask, What might have become of the pig if the Gosky Patties *had* occurred? But we are given no hint . . . except in the terrible word, "Patties.") If we had feelings about the pig, this would not be fun for us. I believe that feelings, *attached* feelings that is, are also dead weight in a poem. We mustn't be feeling things for the poor tethered pigs in poems; poems are to liberate our feelings rather than to bind them. If a poem sticks you to it, it has failed. Consider the example of the death of Lesbia's sparrow, as described by Catullus, that "has hopped solitarily / down that dark alleyway of no return." Our sentiments are stuck neither to the bird nor to Lesbia's grief over its death, but, through Catullus's tone of mock gravity, are connected to something truly grave: that implacable force that "swallows up all beautiful things" (*The Poems of Catullus*, translated by Peter Whigam).

9. INDIFFERENCE TO OUTCOME. There is no product (quite likely), and this is perfectly satisfactory. "If it does not then [turn into Gosky Patties], it never will; and in that case the Pig may be let loose, and the whole process may be considered as finished." There were expectations, it was important to have expectations, but achieving them doesn't matter a black pin. Isn't this the burden of Cavafy's "Ithaca" as much as "Gosky Patties"? Although I hate to bring in the word *burden*; the burden here is that there is no burden. I love this blessed release from the goal. I love the feeling of deflation, in general, that one enjoys in nonsense. Take this familiar rhyme:

> Pussycat, Pussycat, where have you been?
> I've been up to London to visit the Queen.
> Pussycat, Pussycat, what did you there?
> I frightened a little mouse under her chair.

I love the small thing that results from great circumstances. The pussycat goes the long way around to do something she could have done in the next room. When any child repeats this nonsense rhyme she most likely pays no attention to what she's saying, but some interior overworked overdutiful overintentional windup machinery inside her is relaxed, and that is why this rhyme has lasted without anyone ever worrying about it.

10. FRUSTRATION OF ORDINARY EXPECTATIONS. We do not expect "recipes" to fail. Recipes don't just wander off like cattle—or pigs. There will always be a transformation of the ingredients into something else. But that's the fun here; the only transformation is that one is amused whereas one had not been amused. The same argument might be made for contemporary liberties with the sonnet, that their pleasure is somehow bound up with their wandering off from the form.

11. A WONDERFUL SENSE OF HELPLESSNESS. We can do certain (very exact) things to make Gosky Patties, but we have no control over whether or not they *work*. This of course is the exact delicate state required of poetry writing. We can urge parts (pins, cheese, etc.) together and then we have to hope that they will do their part, somehow becoming active in an enterprise that is beyond us.

12. THE OBJECT IS DELIGHT. Lear is first delighting himself and then his audience. And I would argue that the poet as well as the nonsense writer is delighted by his work, whatever the apparent extremity he may be describing in a poem. Could Hopkins, for example, have been anything but delighted/released by the phrase "time's eunuch"? Somehow he created an atomic broth (cooked over despair) that twisted these unlikely word partners together into a supremely powerful and economical description of supreme powerlessness and waste. He is, in the moment of calling himself "time's eunuch," released from *being* "time's eunuch." I wouldn't be at all surprised if he actually laughed. I don't think it would be a rueful laugh, either; it would be joy.

III: MODIFY THE GLEE

I can't go on any longer without reference to Emily Dickinson, whose work is so buoyed by nonsense that it fairly pops out of the water. When I was first thinking about this relationship between poetry and nonsense I opened my copy of Johnson's edition of the *Complete Poems* to find an example in her work, and the book fell open to a remarkable demo poem that I hadn't previously known. But the truth is, when you're reading closely, almost any poem can be a great demo poem. Almost any random poem by a great poet can become your private key to their Enigma machine; although the Enigma machine keeps spitting out different daily codes, you will sense the same deep gizmo behind it. For example, everything in Frost has that same ominous something-that-drains-away-the-gold, once you've really seen it at work in "Nothing Gold Can Stay."

But here is Emily Dickinson's "The Morning after Woe" (#364) :

> The Morning after Woe—
> 'Tis frequently the Way—
> Surpasses all that rose before—
> For utter Jubilee—
>
> As Nature did not care—
> And piled her Blossoms on—
> And further to parade a Joy
> Her Victim stared upon—
>
> The Birds declaim their Tunes—
> Pronouncing every word
> Like Hammers—Did they know they fell
> Like Litanies of Lead—

On here and there—a creature—
They'd modify the Glee
To fit some Crucifixal Clef—
Some Key of Calvary—

Emily Dickinson is a natural in thinking about the cool, ungummifying effects of nonsense on poetry and the liberation nonsense introduces to the spirit. "The Morning after Woe" is a grief-giddy poem, dazzled with loss and filled with extreme invention.

The first two stanzas establish one of those big contrasts so characteristic of Emily Dickinson's way of constructing a poem, how she rubs rough opposites together so that each side aggravates the other. In this poem the contrast is between the night of woe (probably someone's death) and the tauntingly joyous morning after.

It's the last two stanzas I want to get to. Emily Dickinson's sensitivity this morning (if we agree to think of her as writing this on the morning after a death) is so extreme that the language is exaggerated and speeded up and *cartoonlike*. The mind is impatient with anything local. It has to find some sort of movers— like the little cast-metal car or boot of the Monopoly board—that can maneuver free of the clingy stuff of the actual unbearable morning. She finds birds. She describes the birds as "Pronouncing every word / Like Hammers." See how fast she's moving here from the aural to the physical. She barely slows down as she passes from the sound of birdsong to the still logically related sound of ringing hammers, to the strange shift in logic whereby she keeps the hammer idea, but moves from their sound to their terrible downward weight. The picture is comically impossible; if you think of the birdsong broadcast out (as of a sprinkler, say), it suddenly condenses, going south fast and hard, falling as "Litanies of Lead." The transmutation from the immaterial sound to the aggressively material hammerheads shifts the poem to a cartoon scene where "here and there—a creature" is getting bonked on the head like Krazy Kat.

Now the game changes again. No more weight; back to abstraction. If the birds knew the painful effect their joyous song was having on the sufferers below, "They'd modify the Glee." And it's little wonder the word "glee" should come up here; it's glee that's cranking up this poem, delivering it now to another kind of invention dear to nonsense writers, the invented word,

"Crucifixal," nestled against an actual word: the birds would find some other way of singing, some *Crucifixal Clef*." With that, Emily Dickinson has invented a whole new musical notation—a new pitch of suffering.

Well, no, not suffering. We are far beyond suffering here. We are in the grip of invention so free that invention invents further, so that the first great trope, nudged by the appetites of rhyme ("Glee") effortlessly discovers its own restatement: "Some Key of Calvary." This whole new notational Golgotha at which we arrive is a place discoverable only by language operating on language. The direction of this poem is one of increasing exaggeration and extremity, moving out and out—much as Frost's "Nothing Gold Can Stay"—to a condition of understanding which only the poem sustains. In Frost, we know a shivering gold, in Dickinson this painless pitch beyond hearing. I have to think they were both having a wonderful time.

Nonsense exists only in relation to sense. It uses the rules of sense but comes to different conclusions. What is it but nonsense that has taken the grave weight of Frost's and Dickinson's poems—the sensible, express-ible weight of them: all that is new is soon lost; human grief finds no sympathy in nature—and has left them weightless? Because if these poems, or a Shakespeare sonnet or a Holy Sonnet by Donne, had not had their arguments undone somehow, they would indeed crash upon our heads like hammers.

All feelings must go through the chillifier for us to feel them in that aesthetically thrilling way that we do in poetry. Poetry's feelings are not human feelings; we know the difference. There is some deep exchange of heat for cool that I'm trying to get at, something that I see operating in nonsense and that I believe gives poetry much of its secret irresistibility and staying power (we are not exhausted by it and must always revisit it). In fact I am sure this mysterious exchange informs all the arts I'm drawn to. Today, again, I've found evidence of it in a *New York Times* article about a puppet theater version of Anne Frank's diary ("Puppet Show With Dark Tale to Tell: Anne Frank's," January 25, 2006). The puppets are Barbie-sized "pose-able mannequins" that two actresses move around in "a giant cutaway dollhouse, an exact replica of the annex rooms where Anne and her family hid." This unlikely production, which "sounds at first blush like someone's idea of a bad joke," succeeds. It is thought to succeed "because puppets, by their very woodenness, force the audience to fill in movements, expressions and interior lives."

We swarm to a vacuum. We warm a vacuum. That's nonsense; vacuums can't conduct heat. That's funny.

Derichment

Although I want to write about derichment, I recognize the danger: derichment is an idea—*idea* is too pale—that informs every part of my life. It is the story of my life, its occupation, its goal. To speak of it I must separate it from myself, unweave it from my genetic strands. Derichment is my secret; I will give away my secret.

On the other hand, experience has proven that it is almost impossible to give away secrets. Even when I write them down as clearly as I can, people seem to receive another secret, which is secret from me. I like that. And that's not all: *my own secrets can become secret from me again.* Which is to say, having exposed them as best I can—in a poem, say—the secrets remain there, to be visited but not carried away. It is as though I had never whispered them, I am so little changed by what the poem knows. This already has to do with the wonderful processes of derichment, the incalculable mystery by which the world does not grow heavier through its own efforts.

Derichment is a stern faith, according to which it is insufficient to say that the left hand does not know what the right hand is doing; the left hand must also not know what the *left hand* is doing. This, of course, is an ideal, and not fully attainable. Yet one must hold such banners aloft, stitched in gold upon a field of gold. For there are powerful enemy banners, banners reading Profit from Experience! And The Unexamined Life Is Not Worth Living!

But I am getting ahead of myself. Let me begin again. The actual word *derichment* recently presented itself to my mind in reaction to the word *enrichment*. I have always bristled at the idea of enrichment. Children, it is often maintained, must be enriched; bread must be enriched. Weren't they rich already? That is my big question: Weren't they rich already? Wouldn't you have to degrade them somehow in order to make them need enrichment?

But here is derichment in practice, not in theory.

Derichment: The Early Years
In my first year of college, my English teacher, Miss Foley, having confessed herself worn down by the dimness of the previous semester's Intro to Lit students, told

us that although Emily Dickinson was listed on the syllabus, she might skip her our semester, explaining that Dickinson's poetry was very important to her and that she just couldn't go through the brutalization again so soon. She said this quietly. Miss Foley was a forbidding and fascinatingly undemonstrative person. I remember her dry one-*heh* laugh, as though a small seed had stuck in the back of her throat. I also remember the strange Mondrianish business that occupied her hands during her otherwise gesture-free lectures: every few minutes she would look down and rearrange the two or three little stacks of books and papers on her desk, perhaps shifting them from corner to corner, perhaps turning one rectangle perpendicular to another—always unconsciously tidying up, already preparing to leave.

Preparing to leave! Miss Foley had a private life of the mind that she protected, and to which she was eager to return. She wasn't entirely there for us. This absence was maddeningly attractive. In no time I had my hands on the college library's copy of the exciting new Johnson edition of Emily Dickinson (Miss Foley had let this information slip).

Here we see the carrot method of instruction at its least impure. The student was not offered a carrot; at most we might attempt to purify ourselves to the point that we might be worthy of being in the same room with a carrot. This is one of the faces of derichment. There are others.

Elvis Presley

In the summer of 1969, as my then husband and I were driving up to the Canadian Rockies, Elvis Presley came on the radio, singing "Don't Cry Daddy." As I listened to the lyrics, the pines passing by the car windshield began to warp and blur through my tears. It didn't matter a bit that the lines were predictable saccharine sentimental emotionally exploitative poshlost.

I understood with a great shock that the controlling part of me could not distinguish this Elvis-induced emotion from the emotion that attached to profound literature. I hated that. But on the other hand, it was new information—and information I could trust because I didn't want it. This, for me, formative Elvis moment simultaneously demonstrates two major functions of derichment:

1. Hierarchies of sensibilities are a joke
2. Real news only travels through resistance

Sometime Later

When my mother, near the end of her life, inherited sixty thousand dollars from her San Francisco aunt, there were only a few things she could think of to want. She got a newer used car, moving up from a big cruiser of a 1960 Chevy to a more maneuverable later-model Dodge Dart. And she got a brand-new television with a screen modestly larger than her old one; in a mobile home you can't back up far enough for a really big screen. Then I quit hearing about her getting anything else new. Pretty soon I asked her if she was treating herself to some of the luxuries she could now afford. She said, "Oh, I tried canned salmon, but to tell you the truth I like tuna just as much."

I got such a kick out of that; such a stunted idea of luxury, I thought. I repeated that story for years to give an idea of my mother. There was also a companion story, about when we'd go to the Basque restaurant out on the same highway that the trailer park was on. The traditional Basque dinner had lots of courses, many more than my mother was used to. She enjoyed it all, the chilled red wine, the iceberg lettuce salad, the marinated tongue, the minestrone, the basket of French bread with butter pats, the family-style bowl of red beans, the bowl of French fries, eventually the main course of two pork chops or lamb chops or slices of prime rib, and then ice cream. At the end of dinner she could be counted on to say, "You know, I could have just filled up on the beans."

There are several things here to enjoy, and to admire. First, tested by wealth, tested by variety, my mother's pleasures remained her pleasures. It was not as though she was a shrunken-up person without the capacity for pleasure; she had liked things very well right along—things like tuna and beans. And when presented with other delicious choices, she still liked tuna and beans. It is pleasant to think of a person like that, who genuinely likes what she has. It is also pleasant for a person to be so predictable, to say the same thing over and over as she did. There are ways in which pleasures become deeper when they are repeated. This is bedrock derichment stuff.

The Grand Canyon

The human chest can tolerate quite a lot of canyon, but finally there is a quantity of canyon from which one must turn away, and surely that is the Grand Canyon. This explains why it is so overphotographed. When a person comes to the lip of what she cannot hope to embrace, she is likely to take a picture of it. This makes perfect sense. The picture will capture what she cannot, and therefore, in a magical way, the too-great will not be lost. We have many such methods of convincing ourselves that we have embraced things that in truth defy us. We have big libraries of photographs and videotapes that we hope are holding onto things until we can get back to them.

"Free, Quiet and Alone"

A great agent of derichment is enforced bed rest. Many of the distractions to which one is susceptible upon getting up do not visit the bed.

Although perhaps, upon further reflection, it isn't only the bed that advances derichment; perhaps if one remained anywhere without being able to shift, the same benefit would obtain. Consider, for example, the great Portuguese poet Fernando Pessoa's assistant book-keeper's desk, his torment, his liberation.

But it is Matisse's bed that has presented itself to my mind. Matisse was apparently an ordinary boy. By twenty he had become a law clerk and showed exceptional promise for nothing other than remaining one. Then came the appendicitis operation. To amuse him during his long convalescence, Matisse's mother gave him a paint set and a how-to-paint book. While painting, Matisse felt, as he had never felt before, "free, quiet and alone."

The rest, of course, is *histoire*. But I wanted to underscore the importance of external limitation here. It is the vacuum created by being denied his usual occupations that allowed Matisse the discovery of his deepest self.

Through an act of gratuitous symmetry, Matisse's great career ended with his again being restricted to bed and again finding liberation through limitation. With painting now denied him, he turned to scissors and colored paper to create the dazzling cutouts by which he changed the face of art once more.

It can be a good thing, then, to feel trapped, cut off, at your wit's end, bored silly, left out, tricked, drained. We need to hear that gurgle when the straw probes futilely for more Coke. We need to be deriched.

I Go to AWP

A LIFETIME OF PREFERRING NOT TO

I have always understood myself to be a person who does not go to writers' conferences.

It's been a point of honor: the whole cooperative workshopping thing, not for *me*. I have never *taken* a creative writing class, I have never *taught* a creative writing class, and I have never *gone*, and will never *go*, to anything like AWP, I have often said.

Once, when I was about twenty-five and not yet entirely aware of the extremity of my unclubbability, I did try to go to a writer's conference. Thirty minutes into the keynote address I had a migraine. It turns out I have an aversion to cooperative endeavors of all sorts. I couldn't imagine making a play or movie, for instance; so many people involved. I don't like orchestral music. I don't like team sports. I love the solitary, the hermetic, the cranky self-taught. Make mine the desert saints,

the pole-sitters, the endurance cyclists, the artist who
paints rocks cast from bronze so that they look exactly
like the rocks they were cast from; you can't tell the
difference when they're side by side. It took her years
to do a pocketful. You just know she doesn't go to art
conferences. Certainly not zillion-strong international
ones, giant wheeling circuses of panel discussions.

How, then, one wonders, can it be that I have just
come back from AWP's* annual conference in Vancouver, treading upon a lifetime of preferring not to?

IT WAS EASIER THAN I THOUGHT

I was invited to attend as an outsider, and to write a
piece for *Poetry*. I could go but retain my alienation. This
was so doable. Of course, in truth I could only do this
now, when I am quite old. If I were young and hadn't
published anything, it would be different. Now, even
if my sense of my self is threatened, shouldn't I already
have used most of it up? How much more can there
be left? Maybe I would never have been influenced,
as I feared I would, but to this day I believe I needed

---

* Association of Writers and Writing Programs

to guard against *something*, even if that something was imaginary. I needed to protect something valuable. The most important thing a beginning writer may have going for her is her bone-deep impulse to defend a self that at the time might not look all that worth getting worked up about. You'll note a feral protectiveness—a wariness, a mistrust. But the important point is that this mistrust is the *outside* of the place that has to be kept empty for the slow development of self-trust. You have to defend before it looks like you have anything *to* defend. *But if you don't do it too early, it's too late.*

One must truly HOLD A SPACE for oneself. All things conspire to close up this space. Everything about AWP has always struck me as closing the space.

ANOTHER FEAR

I have a weak character. I am very susceptible to other people's enthusiasms, at times actually courting them. I like to sit among people who feel strongly about a basketball team, say, and get excited with them. I love to love ouzo with ouzo lovers. These are, of course, innocent examples. But this weakness concerns me in going to AWP. If I'm exposed to the enthusiasms of others, I know that I am capable of betraying my deepest convictions, laughing in the face of a lifetime of hostility to instruction, horror at groupthink. The only way I've ever gotten along in this world is by staying away from it; I have had only enough character to keep myself out of situations that require character. Now here I am, going to AWP. How am I going to remember: these people are THE SPAWN OF THE DEVIL? They will seem like individuals, not deadly white threads of the great creative writing fungus.

REGISTRATION

Wednesday, March 30, 2005

I am given a black tote bag when I register. Very nice with the AWP logo. I see on a table behind the registration station hundreds of these black bags, primed with schedules, and stacked up like gunnysacks at the potato packers. The schedule is a 230-page affair. I note with rising alarm that there are up to fifteen choices for what to do each hour-and-a-half session, morning to night, for three days.

What we have here before us is the exhilaration of *bulk*: bulk bags, bulk panels, bulk poets. Even though this is Canada, we are having an American experience: the American romance with bulk. Attendees who use American institutions such as Costco won't have a problem. They already know how to handle things like AWP. They already know about proportion. A Costco sense of proportion is understanding that you have to get enough bulk to fill up your pickup-bed-sized shopping cart. And you have to have that shopping cart (which will hold four steel-belted radials) because regular-sized ones would look miniature in proportion with the wide avenues of the towering metropolis of bulk. Everything conspires to shame you out of any natural modesty you came in with. You cannot just want a bottle of Tabasco sauce.

Any more than you could just want to go to one panel or hear one writer read.

The AWP catalog says to you, as the Costco shopping cart says to you, Think big! Glut yourself! All this wouldn't be going on if it weren't a good idea to heap your day up with it! And don't worry; it's all disposable! One panel will wipe out all memory of the previous panel, just like with TV. It would be wrong, unthrifty, to go back to your room and sit.

Plus, as with Costcos, which are inevitably situated a long way from wherever you live, you have come so far, all the way to Canada! You'd better fill up.

THE BOOKFAIR

Because this is only Wednesday, registration day, most of the tables in the big hall are still empty, but there are signs announcing the names of the presses and journals that will be occupying them. There are venerable names and new ones. Some of these journals I've had dealings with for decades. Slow dealings, sending off poems in the mail, waiting for a reply. By the time I'd get my poems back (usually all of them) they would look new to me. I could see them in a new way, maybe like children getting off the bus from their first day of school. They'd been somewhere where they had had to fend for themselves. You could get a new respect for them, and also you could think to yourself, How could I have sent them off looking like that?

In any case, it was a distant, silent relationship with these presses and journals. I wanted something from them, but I had to count on the words I'd put on the page to get it for me. Whether or not I started out liking the patient discipline of this exchange, I came to like it. It slowed me down. If I'd gotten those poems back at email speed, say, they wouldn't have been away long enough for me to lose hope the way you need to. You really shouldn't be living for a reaction all the time.

I also liked the fact that there were no faces or voices; we were all disembodied, writer and editor alike. Just the slow old mail. I wanted my poems to fight their way like that. Fight and fight again. No networking, no friends in high places, no internships. I think that's how poems finally have to live, alone without your help, so they should get used to it.

Tomorrow morning at the AWP bookfair a young writer will be able to meet everybody, editors, publishers, all in one place. They'll all be sitting there behind their piles of books and journals. The hopeful young writer could have conversations, exchange email addresses, hand them manuscripts. Next month if he sent an editor some work he could start his email with, "I'm following up on our conversation at last month's AWP bookfair . . ." It kind of makes me sick to think about.

On the other hand, maybe there will be free key chains.

THE CONFERENCE BEGINS

My First Panel Experience

Thursday, March 31
9:00–10:15 AM

"The Creative Process: The Creative Writer as Teacher"
I'm sitting in the Vancouver Island Room on the conference floor of the Fairmont Hotel. The draped and elevated table of the panel setup looks like the Last Supper but just with water glasses. The room is aggressively paneled in white with elaborate gold trim. Even the chandeliered ceiling is paneled and trimmed. Good motif for panels, I guess.

The question to be addressed by our panel is, How does the creative writing teacher stay creative? I have chosen this panel using my current selection method: What looks most inimical to your nature?

These creative writing teachers have apparently gone into this line of work because they felt themselves helped by a writing teacher and feel a desire to pass it on. They resort frequently to various forms of the word "mentor," both noun and verb. They share a meaning for this word so that it requires no explanation.

Nor are they confused by the verb *to workshop*. As easily and comfortably as I might say, "We started *sanding* the table" do these creative writing teachers say, "We started *workshopping* poems."

Before we get to the question of how the creative writing teacher might stay creative, I would like to pause at these words, *mentor* and *workshop*. If, as my dictionary tells me, a *mentor* is a wise counselor, then *to mentor* would surely be to give wise counsel. And of course it would imply somebody on the other side receiving the wise counsel. Because it seems to me so deep and intimate, I have always had a very cautious feeling about this word *mentor*, as something far beyond the teacher of a class a student signed up for. It would be specific to two people who found some particular affinity, a relationship that would develop gradually. It would rarely occur.

When I was a young writer, for some years I only knew one poet, Rosalie Moore, thirty-plus years my senior. We got to be friends and she was encouraging to me, but we barely understood each other. We stayed friends until she died in her nineties. Occasionally over the years someone would refer to Rosalie as my mentor and I always felt an electric shock, like red cartoon arrows flying off my body, like bristles. Rosalie wasn't my mentor. She would agree with that. I just don't think the word should be used casually. It should be deep. Some people have mentors, some never do. I didn't.

Workshop. In the old days before creative writing programs, a workshop was a place, often a basement, where you *sawed* or *hammered*, *drilled* or *planed* something. You could not simply *workshop* something. Now you can, though. You can take something you wrote by yourself to a group and get it workshopped. Sometimes it probably is a lot like getting it hammered. Other writers read your work, give their reactions, and make suggestions for change. A writer might bring a piece back for more workshopping later, even. I have to assume that the writer respects these other writers' opinions, and that just scares the daylights out of me. It doesn't matter if their opinions really are respectable; I just think the writer has given up way too much inside. Let's not share. Really. Go off in your own direction way too far, get lost, test the metal of your work in your own acids. These are experiments you can perform down in that old kind of workshop, where Dad used to hide out from too many other people's claims on him.

BACK TO THE PANEL

The ways the panel members say they stay creative are not what I would have said in their place, which is that I abandoned the teaching of creative writing and ran as though my clothes were on fire. Rather, one says she teaches but she also does her own writing projects at the same time, currently putting together an anthology of stories by sex workers. This is a person of an industry, social responsibility, and generosity beyond my imagining. A number of panel members, with members of the audience nodding in agreement, say that they are actually *nourished* by student work, and stimulated to do their own work. I am speechless. My sense of this panel, mostly made up of women and attended by women for what reason I can't say, is that these are sincere, helpful, useful people who show their students their own gifts and help them to enjoy the riches of language while also trying to get some writing done themselves. They have to juggle these competing demands upon their souls and it is hard and honorable. I agree, and shoot me now.

RECONSIDERATION: NEGLECTED AND FORGOTTEN POETS

10:30–11:45 AM

A different room
I already feel stunned, absent, polite, and I'm just starting my second panel. I saw Margaret Kaufman from Marin in the jam-packed wood-paneled elevator coming down to the conference floor, all of us with tags around our necks and black totes. I was embarrassed to be seen. She invited me to join her and Jackie Kudler for dinner. I made vague distracted sounds.

This is a big, big room, with big, big chandeliers and really lots of paneling. I didn't get a copy of the handout of the poems; all gone.

Ignored poet #1: John Logan. Presenter mumbled and did not raise his eyes. I take personal offense at this sort of behavior. He also didn't introduce himself. What is it with that?

These presenters assume that everybody has taken/ taught writing courses. It's natural life to everyone here. They refer to their own professors and various writing programs where they've taught or been students, and the audience murmurs, laughs, and groans in response, because that's the kind of church this is. Obviously, this is a big part of the pleasure of a conference like this, the Good Sam Club quality, the fact that these people kind of know each other; they migrate all over the continent, not in trailers, but nonetheless as a fluid band, dividing, reforming. Tagged, like birds.

Do the presenters not introduce themselves because they are modest? Because they expect to be known? Because the previous presenter didn't?

I notice that these ignored poets tend to be unearthed by their old students. No surprise there, I guess.

". . . creative process that reflects dialectical [mumble] . . ." Blurry speakers, reading essays of routine critical phrasing . . .

(I guess I shouldn't have expected to like neglected poets since I don't like many unneglected ones even.)

". . . relation between gnostic and experiential truth . . ."

I hear furious clapping from some other room; I feel I have come to the wrong panel.

THE AMERICAN SONNET

12:00–1:15 PM, that same day

My third panel in one morning! I'm off to a strong start.

About a hundred people are waiting to hear about the American sonnet. The room is stuffed. That itself is something, don't you think? A hundred people would choose the sonnet panel over the fourteen other panels on offer this session, ranging from "Women Writing Obsession and the Twenty-First-Century Imagination" to "Where It's All Too Real: Alaska's Nonfictional Demand." It's enough to make you think that maybe people interested in poetry are hungry for some order, some shared requirements. It's moving to me. Most of the scheduled panelists don't show up, including Gerald Stern, whom everyone misses a lot because of the way he is in person (I don't know how he is) and because of his apparently freewheeling approach to the sonnet.

Molly Peacock is a late-add to the decimated panel, but she says a nice thing. She says it's wrong to think of the sonnet as a "container," or prison; instead it is a "skeleton," which allows something to live and move. I can see a beautiful animated x-ray of a galloping horse. This is a muscular and vigorous feeling about form. And in addition to the form's usefulness as an armature, Peacock recommends the writing of sonnets as a way to measure oneself against the history of literature, and a way to *connect* with that history. Whatever one's feelings about sonnet writing, I find these attractive thoughts, after so many years of everybody going it so damned alone. Wanting to be connected, wanting to be great in some great tradition, these are sweet ideas. But how can I reconcile them with my own preference for isolation from the other toilers? I explain it to myself this way: I don't want to be connected to poetry in an easy, fellowshipping way, but I *do* want to be connected in a way that will earn me the respect of the dead.

LUNCH BREAK

I met up with Dorianne Laux at the sonnet panel. In spite of my abstract contempt for everyone in attendance here, I am on the functional level delighted as well as grateful to see this person whom I know and like, a warm human

being, a strong poet, and the head of a writing program
in Oregon. This is all so distressing. I knew it would be.
We find Dorianne's husband, world's-nicest-poet Joe
Millar, and collect Major Jackson, a young poet making
a name for himself, teaching in a writing program, and
not incidentally an old student of Dorianne's, and we all
go for lunch at a little place around the corner from the
Fairmont. I am so happy to be tucked into this booth
with these down-to-earth, generous people whose lives
are writing, as mine is. Why have I kept myself from this
camaraderie? There's lots of relaxed book chat. Major
talks about not yet feeling he has an *arc* for his new book.
(What *is* an arc? Dorianne explains that this is a term
current in creative writing circles and refers to a shape
the whole book of poems should ideally have, like a
narrative arc, as I understand it, and forgive me if I have
this wrong.) Already it is coming to me why I don't
have more of this camaraderie; just the thought of vogue
shapes for poetry books oppresses like cathedral tunes.
Dorianne seems to be able to coexist with stuff like this,
letting it wash over her. The more I think about it, the
more oppressed I feel—so many of us writing books of
poetry, with or without *arc*. How in the world can I feel
really, really special? No, I think poets should take the

lesson of the great aromatic eucalyptus tree and poison the soil beneath us.

THE CONTEMPORARY SESTINA

3:00–4:15 PM, still that same day somehow

I can't stay away from these panels on forms. Just to say "the contemporary sestina" sounds as lovely and hopeless as saying "the contemporary minuet."

And again, there is a full house. I will admit to having no personal patience with using such an extremely strict form (or indeed any strict forms) but I feel an attraction to the general atmosphere of rigor it excites. It feels penitential, religious in its extremity, the sestina: a scourge against shapelessness, a six-sextet-plus-a-tercet rod of discipline.

And indeed the panelists quickly establish an atmosphere of almost kabalistic mystery for the antique sestina, which had its heyday in the Middle Ages. We are plunged immediately into its spiritual possibilities. When we enter it, do we leave worldly time and enter ecstatic eternal time? Is the sestina another form of the medieval cathedral? Does the numerologically suggestive sestina allow entrance into the *axis mundi?* Perhaps the sestina—because of the ways it repeats—is an uroboros (accent on the *second* syllable, I note) eating its tail, cycling without end. And this question arises: Can a ritual (the form of the sestina, for example) be somehow satisfying in itself, even if we no longer understand why it has the pattern it has or what powers it was originally meant to invoke? Can the repetition of a pattern—alone—give us consolation? I cannot speak about the sestina particularly, but in general I think, yes; we are adjusted, physically *corrected*, by the repetition of patterns. They hit some deep drone part of our brains and make things better.

But to return to the sestina: it is especially good for obsessive-compulsives, say the practitioners (both kidding and not), perfect for those who enjoy being "boxed in." The sestina says over and over, "You must say it some other way" (other than the easy way). The sestina-writer creates her own monster as she battles it, the meanings of the six repeated words twisting and writhing away as the dragon of the sestina grows sextet by sextet. I enjoy the panel's emphasis on what a titanic wrestling match it is to write a poem. I certainly feel this when I write a poem, even though it's not a sestina.

What a fine panel this panel was, inviting the mystical by way of stringent form, celebrating at once the exercise of intention and the fruitful thwarting of intention. I felt completely removed from the modern world.

WHERE ARE THE POET-CRITICS?

Friday, April 1 (hump of the conference)
9:00–10:15 AM

Herb Leibowitz, who edits *Parnassus*, was supposed to be on this panel, and I really wanted to meet him. He edited an essay of mine for his magazine once, and he was so fussy that it seemed like a grooming ritual from another hemisphere, important in ways that I couldn't understand. I hoped all the people on this panel would be smart and particular like that.

Herb Leibowitz didn't show, but the present speaker seemed to fit the bill. I had come in quite late, I'm sorry to say (panel hangover from yesterday), and the room was excitingly jammed, people sitting on the floor, a hundred and fifty, maybe two hundred, in all. There was a smart feeling here. The severely dressed woman to my left, taking furious notes in her Moleskine as I snuck into the last free seat, would not deign to tell me that it was Linda Gregerson speaking although I whispered my inquiry. It was my shoddy behavior of arriving late and wanting to be caught up. I hate that too.

Linda Gregerson spoke of the importance of the poet–critic in a precise and strenuous manner that I appreciated very much. It's satisfying to watch someone being exact in front of you. It makes you automatically feel that what they are saying matters. There was a compelling, hesitating quality to her sentences, as though in each she was rejecting a variety of possible formulations, very quickly, before fastening upon the happiest. We have to listen to so many dumb people; it's such a pleasure to watch somebody's brain working that fast. A second panel member, Cynthia Hogue, was also compelling, but not in that close-cropped-hair way I especially like. Hers was a more relaxed-haired intelligence. She spoke of having bought the whole deconstructionist thing of the eighties and of having adopted its alienating jargon. At the time she found it intellectually exhilarating plus she had to get her PhD. It had taken her years, she said, to purge her language of this theoretical luggage and to come to understand that criticism and poetry should talk. I like this very sophisticated AA confession thing, confessing to being a reformed deconstructionist. I am failing to get across the high level of discourse this panel was at, but it was a high level. It appears that the theoretical zealotry of the eighties is in major decline and it's getting to be OK for all sorts of good sense to reign again. This was a serious and passionate gathering. Cynthia Hogue said, and it thrills me when someone will go this far: "Critical writing is spiritual practice." Of course it is. Everything truly attended to is spiritual practice, isn't it? More of that, please.

TRANSGRESSIVE AND POST-CONFESSIONAL NARRATIVE IN CONTEMPORARY AMERICAN POETRY

12:00–1:15 PM

Such a lot to think about, just in the panel's title!

The word *transgressive* is thick upon the ground here at AWP. I could also have attended panels titled, "Transgression and Convention: Writing the Erotic Poem" and "Impure Poetry: The Poetics of the Transgressive, Taboo, and Impolite." It's funny how writers will all want to jump on the same bed till the springs pop out. Then they go jump on another one. Transgressive apparently means sex now. Didn't there used to be other transgressions? Will there be others again?

How about, transgression against obsessive self-regard? That would be a good one: "Hello. I'm Jen and I keep having impersonal thoughts."

Then *post-confessional*. What could this mean? Is post-confession what comes *after* confession? Perhaps contrition? Or Hail Marys? Or dedication to good works? Or does post-confessional mean confessional like Sexton or Lowell, but ironic and self-conscious now—saying, I am confessing, I see myself confessing, but I know no one can really confess?

In the event, transgressive and post-confessional narrative turned out to mean loosely plotted tales of sex and attitude, read really fast and/or at high volume, which left me feeling amused and pleasantly avuncular, grateful to not be listening to a mumble panel.

Wait; *I* can't feel avuncular. I'm a genetic *woman*. But I *do*. Am I starting to have *transgressive issues*?

A DRINK IN THE BAR

Friday night and none too soon

I met up with someone I knew, a longtime magazine editor not used to AWP and as ill at ease as I was. We had a drink in the bar of the Fairmont. I'd already had a drink there earlier and had set my backpack on fire in the candle on the low table between the cozy chairs. Big flames. I was wise to that this time. The editor hated being there. He knew it was going to make his life harder; every writer you meet means one more personal rejection letter you have to write. We both resented, but from opposite ends, personality horning in on the real question: the words on the page.

TELLING SECRETS, LOUD SILENCES, AND CONSENSUAL REALITY: THE ART OF THE MEMOIR

Saturday, April 2
1:30–2:45 PM

Phillip Lopate, etc.
My last panel!

I went to this because I love Phillip Lopate's essay anthology so much.

Memoir is the perfect thing to hear talked about or read aloud. You can stand lots and lots (as opposed to poetry). It's juicy stories: father with hands cut off,

son bathing him; mentally ill daughter who must constantly tell her life aloud; the brother who married the
Headless Woman in the circus; the father who choked
his wife (but not all the way).

The concern of this panel is, How far can you
go, telling other people's secrets? A tormenting question, and not just legally. The memoirist whose brother
married the Headless Woman, for example, lost good
relations with a sister over her tale-telling.

The audience is very interested. Judging by their
detailed questions to the panelists, they intend to Try
This at Home. Is it fair to write about your young
children? Your still-living parents? I am refreshed by
Phillip Lopate's candor; he is less concerned with being
seen as a good guy and a non-exploiter than he is with
making "something shapely." I think it's good to admit
what a wolfish thing art is; I trust writers who know
they aren't nice.

BRIEF DILATION UPON PANELS

There is something inherently Monty Pythonish about
panels. The setup is perfect for farce: starched rigidity
(topic, table, moderator, time limits, matching water

goblets) combined with a thrumming undercurrent of overcivilized competition. Soon after introductions, the dramatic differences in style and talent among the panelists begin to tear the table apart. In the best panels a happy anarchy ensues resulting in a shambles enjoyed by all.

THE BIG FINAL READING

4:30–6:15 PM
(*especially long session—the star treatment*)

Anne Carson and W. S. Merwin
Amazing disorienting mystery room! They have gutted the interior of the conference floor (where I have occupied so many paneled interiors these last three days) to create a single room the size of a sports pavilion for the big final reading. Hundreds and hundreds of AWP attendees drain through the large doors. There is an irresistible pull to this room. I can't calculate the strength it would have taken not to come. Maybe if you were early, it wouldn't be like this; it's probably the great suck of people. Something important must be going to happen if there are this many people here. We are

thousands, maybe a million. We darken the long rows of chairs. We are one organism—a seated organism.

I am pretty far up front, maybe thirty or forty rows back, and Anne Carson is quite big, I mean the top half of her that I can see. She is larger than the top half of a gelcap, maybe a gelcap half and a half. It is easy to make out her black tuxedoish jacket and the blazing white shirt whose collar flies up into dramatic wing tips like a magician's. She is sporting an insouciant brown ponytail! I always thought of her with her hair down and this is much more playful. I can see it bounce when she turns her head suddenly to the side. These are show clothes and this will be a show! I can't see her expressions, but fortunately she has a microphone for expressions. It's hard to judge, when a person is in the gelcap size range, but she seems gamine, elfin. Oh, and really, really smart. How does smart sound? It isn't the Greek and Latin references. The smartness is a tone, something light—dry—exact and amused. It makes it a pleasure to listen to her language and thought experiments; they are offered lightly; you are under no emotional obligation to care. Which of course makes it more possible to do so. Noting what a very big audience it is (as though she hadn't *known* it would be), she begins differently than she had planned. She'll start with a thirteen-second (as I recall) interactive love poem relying upon the audience for a small recitative part. She divides us in half with her tiny commanding arm: this million will say this when I indicate ("What a deal!") and this million will say this ("I'll take it!"). She says her parts, we roar our briefer parts, and we're in cahoots, co-creating (we flatter ourselves to think) a heady ambient smartness. It keeps on like that. She does a bunch of Catullus translations—in which she lobs modern references into classical poems (at one point Catullus looks in the "fridge") the way she lobs Latin into her contemporary stuff—not quite beautiful or exactly amusing, but always out of left field.

W. S. Merwin reads second. Not a fortunate match. We are assured that he has won every prize winnable but it is hard to see why here today. The poems drift across the acres of convention space as vague and shapeless as clouds; I keep feeling like maybe I'm taking mini-naps and missing the pieces that connect things up.

But what could you tell about anybody's poetry anyhow in this big-top atmosphere? The room is all out of proportion with how poetry works. The pressure is all wrong. This place is right for revivals and mass conversions, for stars and demagogues. I don't think I'd trust poetry that worked too well here. Aren't the persuasions of poetry private? To my mind, the right-sized room to hear poetry is my head, the words speaking from the page.

ON THE WAY HOME

It's over.

On the Sunday morning flight back to San Francisco I had the aisle seat next to two young women who, judging by their totes, had been to AWP. Except for serving as a mild obstacle in the passing of snacks, I was invisible to them and their friends seated across the aisle. My seatmates spent much of the flight planning out an elaborate future exchange of poems, something that would spur them to write after they no longer had the support of the creative writing program they were finishing. Near the end of the flight, when it's safe to talk to strangers because you will soon separate, I offered my opinion on the Carson/Merwin reading they'd started discussing, and then we all said who we were. The young woman by the window said, "Wait, are you the Kay Ryan who wrote an essay about becoming a poet? Because I used that essay in the first creative writing class I ever taught, and it worked so well!"

It turned out that she and I wound up waiting at the same Airporter bench, and she said again how happy she was to have met me. Oh God, wasn't this just the perfect illustration of everything I hated? Wasn't this the AWP predicament in miniature? What in the world was this lovely unfledged creature doing teaching a creative writing course? And what in the world was my essay doing encouraging these ever-expanding fuzzy rings of literary mediocrity, deepening the dismal soup of helpful supportive writing environments? Shouldn't I have been up on my back legs as least as much as Simone Weil would have been? Simone Weil, you will recall, abominated all mediocrity and would have recommended vaporizing all of its creators but for the fact that the mediocre grows in the same soil as the great and therefore kill one, kill the other. Simone Weil would have starved herself to death before she would have gone to AWP.

But I had already gone to AWP. And in the presence of this pleasant and possibly promising person waiting for the bus with me I didn't even *think* of vaporizing anything or anybody. No, I didn't even struggle in my chains. Instead I felt pleased that my essay had proven useful, and flattered to be recognized, and wanted very much to be likeable in person.

Specks

While writing a poem the hot wire of thought welds together strange chunks of this and that.

It can't completely combine the disparate elements and make a new element of them, but it can loosen the edges of mutually disinterested materials enough to bond them so that a serial lumpy going-on is achieved, crude emergency bridges made, say, of brush and old doors, just barely strong enough to get the thought across before the furious townspeople show up.

Because thought is stolen, of course, ripped out of a case and carried off in a sack.

Anything nearby is pressed into service to forward the thought. The lathered horse falls out of the picture as the horseman hurls himself and the sack onto the speeding train. When he leaps to a crane, the train falls away, and so on, according to the laws of attention and expedience.

And you will note the presence of "speed" in the middle of expedience: only high speeds permit the transmission of thought, the brief mutations of substance, the continued whispered advance of some articulation which is at once autonomous and at the same time completely the product of what's available to make itself out of.

Thus we cannot separate thought from conversion; we must see the two forces melted into one, thought as conversion itself, and thus never static, never possessable, but like the edges of combustion where the creosote is bubbling to explode in a ripply red line advancing across the desert.

*

It's not so much what poems are, in themselves, but the infinitely larger optimism they offer by their intermittent twinkles: that beneath the little lights on their tiny masts, so far from one another, so lost to each other, there must be a single black sea. We could have no sense of the continuousness of the unknowable without these buoyant specks.

*

The poem is a space capsule in which impossible combinations feel casual. The body of the capsule is of necessity very strong to have broken out of gravity. It is the hard case for the frail experiments inside. Not frail in the wasted sense, but frail in the opposite sense: the brief visibility of the invisible.

*

Because what I am transporting in my hands is both weightless and invisible, and because it must be held loosely, it is impossible to know at the time if I *have* carried it or if what I have done is a comical act, a person *pretending* to carry something carefully; a farcelike delicacy of manners.

*

Some people have one great dream in life which they fail to fulfill.
Others have no dream at all and fail to fulfill even that.
> —Fernando Pessoa

I have a note beside this that says: *ha ha perfect Pessoa.*

Maybe some of us are wired backwards and respond paradoxically to stimuli. Maybe what we think is orange is blue. But I for one have always laughed in the presence of the dismal. Not ruefully but with fresh relish. I cannot tire of Pessoa's *Book of Disquiet* or Larkin's night terrors. They are voluptuaries of the bed of aridity.

★

> Yes, to write is to lose myself, but everyone gets lost, because everything in life is loss. But unlike the river flowing into the estuary for which, unknowing, it was born, I feel no joy in losing myself, but lie like the pool left on the beach at high tide, a pool whose waters, swallowed by the sands, never more return to the sea.
>
> —*Fernando Pessoa*

As distinct as Pessoa is, he is nonetheless one of the category of writers who find themselves and their reactions so far outside the conventional that they have no tools but those they construct for themselves for knowing anything, for finding their bearings. They must synthesize gravity, direction, time, substance. They can't use anyone else's.

It explains these writers completely. It is as though the atmosphere, beautiful and breathable to everyone else, were toxic to them, a poison gas. They are urgently occupied with building a conversion machine. Oh, and this conversion machine can never be finished. Every day it has to be built over again, but differently. To an outside eye, the machines would look identical, but to the poet, panicking for lack of air, something has gone wrong again. It all has to be undertaken again—from scratch.

★

Dust of Snow

The way a crow
Shook down on me
The dust of snow
From a hemlock tree

Has given my heart
A change of mood
And saved some part
Of a day I had rued.

—*Robert Frost*

I have a terrible time remembering anything, so I really appreciate a poem I can hold onto.

But additionally, greatness in a poem can be calculated as the relationship between means and ends: the bigger the disproportion the greater the poem. Which makes "Dust of Snow" ridiculously great. It is one sentence. Only two words go to two syllables.

It doesn't have any metaphors. You could cover it up with a matchbook.

Nothing keeps the poem from being metabolized. The rhymes button perfectly into their buttonholes. The picture is black (crow) white (snow) and utterly simple. That's all there is, out in the snow of the empty page.

So it begins sinking into the mind and turning into our own personal shift: how any little surprise can dislodge everything. A bad day can go on forever; release from it is the putting-right of the universe.

It takes such perfect intuition to know to shut up like this, to know that all you have to do is get the crack started and let the crack continue in the reader.

The amount you need to say is so hard to gauge. How much can you not say, and something will still have the charge of the unsaid? There is a point at which what is said is too pale, or frail, one fears, to tip the mind into the unsaid. And the reason for the pallor might not be punctilio but a genuine failure of force.

But there is no failure of force here. Frost does what needs to be done to make his poem work. And if it takes a minor adjustment to conversational phrasing to get the rhyme, he makes it. I mean, no one would *say* "saved some part of a day I had rued." It's not quite speech.

Frost goes on and on about the "sound of sense," but you notice he'll do what he has to do to make the poem stick in your head. Because above everything else, as he says in his *Paris Review* interview, "you've got to *score*."

And back to the idea that the poem doesn't use any metaphors: of course it is also *only* a metaphor. If it were just a little Vermont stamp we would forget it. No, it's the break-line where the welding of the world comes loose.

★

Reference Back

That was a pretty one, I heard you call
From the unsatisfactory hall
To the unsatisfactory room where I
Played record after record, idly,
Wasting my time at home, that you
Looked so much forward to.

Oliver's *Riverside Blues*, it was. And now
I shall, I suppose, always remember how
The flock of notes those antique Negroes blew
Out of Chicago air into
A huge remembering pre-electric horn
The year after I was born
Three decades later made this sudden bridge
From your unsatisfactory age
To my unsatisfactory prime.

Truly, though our element is time,
We are not suited to the long perspectives
Open at each instant of our lives.
They link us to our losses: worse,
They show us what we have as it once was,
Blindingly undiminished, just as though
By acting differently we could have kept it so.

—*Philip Larkin*

His old mother hovers about, listening from the hall beyond the bedroom where he has ineffectually barricaded himself with his record player. It takes Larkin just six lines to set the trap.

I always want to laugh at the perfection of these setups. We know this desperate stuckness well from his other poems. There could almost be a Chinese character, one single figure that would mean in all its pent-up intensity, "Larkin's fix." He's always in Larkin's fix.

He's such a comically unattractive character. It's a marvel to me that he exposes himself so mercilessly. Another marvel to me is the sleight of hand that Larkin works on us from inside these suffocating chambers, dumping the emotional contents from stanza to stanza, room to room, mother to son, ear to ear, creating a sense of permeability and interpenetration while at the same time walling the poem up with contrary rhetoric. The effect is classic Larkin: irresistible fluidity *completely boxed in*.

"Blindingly undiminished" is sophistry. Things were never as they once were; I mean, even when they were, they weren't. But that doesn't take a thing away from the fact that these terrible nostalgic gusts (to which we are constantly susceptible) feel true. They are made up by us; they are abetted by the lyric temperament; we visit them and suffer phantom perfection.

The quick flash in the dark created by the phrase "blindingly undiminished"—and extinguished by every other line in the poem—is the breeding reactor for the whole thing. It is such an unbearably intense radiation that only a sad sack like Larkin can wrap it in a sufficient number of wet blankets to make it bearable to us.

Again and again it's this threatened *availability* of everything we ever desired that puts the fire under Larkin's kettles. How could we stand his poems otherwise? Why would we?

Today I feel the opposite of Borges, who wished all poetry could be anonymous, or at least his. I want the human trajectory, the feeling of the personal struggle against paralysis and despair and ridiculousness. I want Larkin to fight in his Larkinness. I want him to sneak through the obstacles one more time.

★

Something Matters but We Don't

In man, I can see no substance solidly;
it is as if what we call man were no more
than an oddly angled look at something else.
Or is it my limitation, being man,
not to be able to see whatever is there?
And aren't these two alternatives the same?

Let me leave off speaking, unknowing as I am,
but not before I speak of the limits of speech,
or tell of man that there is nothing to tell,
or tell of what we discern perhaps there could be
to tell that we know too little except it is there
and, if anything happens, it must be it happens there

and not to us, not by us: good
or evil, it doesn't matter what we do.

—*William Bronk*

I was enjoying the grind of Bronk, admiring it this morning.

We are all trying to focus, but we each have a particular distance we care about. Some people are after a granular closeness, some want some middle range. For Bronk, the remoteness is extreme. He's so hungry to get some faraway focus and he just can't. All of his poems are these barren tripod marks, where he set up his glass once again, where he tried again.

I don't know why the evidence of failure should provide consolation but it always does.

★

#1099

My Cocoon tightens—Colors tease—
I'm feeling for the Air—
A dim capacity for Wings
Demeans the Dress I wear—

A power of Butterfly must be—
The Aptitude to fly
Meadows of Majesty concedes
And easy Sweeps of Sky—

So I must baffle at the Hint
And cipher at the Sign
And make much blunder, if at last
I take the clue divine—

—*Emily Dickinson*

Higginson was right; she *is* spasmodic. Dickinson terrain is hard on the brain suspension. In any poem of more than one stanza, one stanza is likely to bottom out.

#1099 has several things not going for it. First, I always worry when it looks like she's going to inhabit an insect. These experiments can go bad in the fey direction. (Recall the "little tippler / leaning against the—sun—") And here she is in stanza one already sensing herself in the early stages of becoming a butterfly.

It's a very odd condition, squeezed into a cocoon while also still in her dress—not fey but off-balance and unsettled. She isn't the one thing or the other quite yet; her condition is conjectural. "Colors tease," and she feels "A dim capacity for Wings." So far the picture's funny and ill fitting and, well, let's just say so, ravishing: it takes massive poetic wings to think of "A dim capacity for Wings."

Then stanza two just isn't very strong, essentially some Dickinson boilerplate to say, Butterflies fly. Of course it is useful for the advancement of her idea, which is that if she *is* to be a butterfly she must get beyond the cocoon stage. And it does serve the purpose of making a bridge to stanza three, which is the stanza for which I have dog-eared this page in Johnson.

Here she works one of her false-reason tricks, starting the stanza with "So," as though what follows will be the result of what has gone before. As though it won't be a cosmic leap. As though she cared about those old stanzas anymore. But this is a different plane. By now she is purely addressing the poet's interior puzzle: How can I move in the direction of what I sense—not as a butterfly, but as a poet?

This is just such a strange capsule of a stanza. I am so interested in her heavy emphasis on clumsiness here, saying it three ways in three lines: she must *baffle* and *cipher* and *make much blunder* if she's ever going to "take the clue divine." She's turning it over and over: the way of the poet is the way of awkwardness and error.

I don't know if I'm getting across what seems rare to me in this. It's the exhilarating unworkability of it: one can *only* blunder into the light, or whatever the "clue divine" is. It's not gradual, or progressive, or accumulative: you don't get better or make fewer blunders, approaching the godhead step by step. Blundering doesn't work, except it does. It can't lead you there, except it's the only way to get there. I will go so far as to hazard that blundering might be *generative*, meaning that rooting around in a haystack long and fruitlessly enough could conceivably *breed a needle*.

★

The Poet Hin

The foolish poet wonders
Why so much honour
Is given to other poets
But to him
No honour is given.

I am much condescended to, said the poet Hin,
By my inferiors. And, said the poet Hin,
On my tombstone I will have inscribed:
"He was much condescended to by his inferiors."
Then, said the poet Hin,
I shall be properly remembered.

Hin—wiping his tears away, I cried—
Your words tell me
You know the correct use of *shall* and *will*.
That, Hin, is something we may think about,
May, may, may, man.

Well yes, true, said Hin, stopping crying then,
Well yes, but true only in part,
Well, your wiping my tears away
Was a part.

But ah me, ah me,
So much vanity, said he, is in my heart.
Yet not light always is the pain
That roots in levity. Or without fruit wholly
As from this levity's
Flowering pang of melancholy
May grow what is weighty,
May come beauty.

True too, Hin, true too. Well, as now: You have gone on
Differently from what you begun.
Yet both truths have validity,
The one meanly begot, the other nobly,
And as each alone glosses over
What the other says, so only together
Have they a full thought to uncover.

—*Stevie Smith*

Why is this so wonderful?

Because it is utterly headstrong and meant to amuse and gratify her own self, meant to keep herself good company and also to console her, and along the way stumbles into some wisdom.

The most beautiful thoughts and feelings can barely settle or they break us. We can't endure more than the briefest visitations. That's the cruel fact. Almost every writer almost always crushes her own work under the weight of thoughts and feelings. Nobody knows how to be light much of the time. Maybe not even the Dalai Lama. Stevie Smith had some natural advantages, a natural distance from conventional behavior.

The only reason it's bearable to know the things she stubs her toe on is the offhand method of arrival and her chronic throwaway "hi-ho" tone. She sends very hot things through the cooling coils of her poems and plays with them in her bare hands. For of course poems must include hot things; if all the hot things are removed the result cannot be poetry since it is the job of poetry to remain open to the whole catastrophe.

In "The Poet Hin" she manages to say things she utterly means:

1. I am condescended to *by my inferiors.*
2. Levity contains pain and weight and beauty.

But these heavy matters enjoy the particular weightlessness conferred on the reader's mind by the assurance that these are the ravings of an individual. The reader of Stevie Smith can never for an instant forget that she is looking through the cockeyes of Stevie Smith. Everything that transpires does so in Stevie Smith's universe, which is not one's own. Meaning, none of the sufferings hurt and none of the pronouncements crowd the mind. Instead, they can be entertained; we can examine them as if they were toys although they are not.

There is nothing so freeing as someone pleasing herself.

Work which pleases itself first just snips so many binding strings in the minds of others.

★

Notes on the Danger
of Notebooks

I.

Almost everything is supposed to get away from us.

This is our grief. As a condition, it doesn't have to be sad. Really, the sadness comes in, the sepia sadness comes seeping in, from keeping what can't be kept anyhow. Many have wept. Many weep. It is exasperating.

It is also tempting, because it is so easy. It is easy to keep a little notebook, to press a few of the blossoms from an individual spring. Once you start thinking like that, it makes perfect sense to go further, to preserve a representative bloom from each plant from every place and season and year you have known. Each is so beautiful and *worthy*.

And this is not untrue; but it is hobbling. Yes, exactly as though a great horse were restrained from running and trampling for joy. There is a kind of dangerous piety to it. The powerful lineaments of the mighty horse are all ignored in the cataloguing of one variegated patch of spring.

Cavalier. We must be somewhat cavalier in this rich historical word's most contemptuous sense. We must run roughshod over what threaten to become memories. For the truth is that memories are indistinguishable from matter in that they can neither be created (despite the claims of vacation brochures) nor destroyed.

You don't have to worry so much about them, in other words. And you will find that you experience a new availability of energy when you give up trying to preserve what preserves itself. You are relieved of a false and debilitating humility and can enter into a roomier frustration, a more generous appreciation of loss.

For of course it is only within the context of loss that anything can be said to be *found.* That seems ridiculously obvious, and yet we struggle against it. And isn't finding, the moment of finding, our supreme thrill? We call it discovery and make much of it, forgetting that it is the gift of loss.

Still, it is as dangerous to cultivate loss as it is to try to stop it through the keeping of notebooks; we are a self-regarding creature and we will watch ourselves losing and become bewitched by our own affecting actions. We are so moved by ourselves. This is natural, but it is distracting. What can we do?

I think we should try to do *something*, try to make something new, try very hard to write a poem, say; desire very much to articulate something that doesn't yet exist, something we don't yet know; try so hard that currents are created in the electric broth of what is not lost but not kept either, currents which draw to the mind the bits of the not-lost and not-kept that join together through the application of great mental force, extreme mental force, in some new and inevitable sequence appropriate to the new realm of the neither lost nor kept. It is incredibly stable when done right.

II.

When Gertrude Stein was at last after so many years of fruitful absence touring and lecturing in the United States, she was a popular sensation in that she was of a piece, a figure round and burrless as a ball, solid, simple, capable of being perfectly, not partially, misunderstood. She could be completely seen and completely heard; she matched herself. Such homogeneity is nearly unbearable for the complicating mind, and the universities where she lectured were full of such minds. After a certain lecture which had as usual bewildered the sober note-takers (the serious people laboring to understand by writing parts down, making decisions about what was important to write down and what wasn't, seeking a pattern in what was said, attempting to get a fix on it—determining its coordinates like an alien craft's) a photographer came up to Stein. He was elated, ravished by what she had been saying. It was no trouble for him to understand as it was for the audience which had come with the intention of understanding rather than with the intention of taking pictures for the local newspaper. His ease was no surprise to Gertrude Stein. The photographer had simply listened and therefore he had understood, since what Gertrude Stein was saying was always simple, plus she repeated it. The serious note-takers couldn't listen and therefore couldn't understand because they were *trying to remember.*

The serious note-takers intended to make sense later of what Gertrude Stein was saying, so they needed to remember the main points of her lecture. They would not have been pleased with the idea that they didn't have to go back to their offices and *make* sense of it because it already *was* sense. One might say that they lacked the humility necessary to listen. One might observe that, paradoxically, what appeared to be submissive behavior on the part of the note-takers, taking notes, was in fact arrogance.

But of course the serious note-takers were not worse people than the photographer. The photographer's humility was no more intentional than the note-takers' arrogance. The humility necessary to listen cannot be achieved head-on, and that is what gave the photographer his edge. He was partly thinking about getting good photographs—about his equipment, about the lighting. He didn't have to concern himself with these professional things very much because they were almost automatic, but a little.

This slight distraction, this slight angle that his job as photographer required, along with the feeling that he was not a professional in the area that Gertrude Stein was talking about, made him more open to what she was saying. He wasn't going to have to summarize her remarks or offer an evaluation. He was just the newspaper photographer.

Isn't it odd to think that in order to listen we must be a little bit relieved of the intention to understand?

This, of course, is the danger of notebooks. They are the devil's bible. They are the books of understanding later.

If you want to understand, it is a good idea not to think of yourself as a professional in the area in which you want to understand; it is just too big a burden. You have to seem to master everything that happens in your professional area. People ask you questions, and they value your answers. You are tempted to take your opinions seriously—sure death to the delicate, translucent stuff they're made of.

We must be careful what we do because we value our actions so highly. Taking notes, the actual physical act of taking them, along with the resulting document in our own words, lends them a spurious importance. It becomes important to us to determine what we meant by that note because we wrote it. We are very self-conscious and therefore we must be vigilant about what we let ourselves see of ourselves. We can see too much.

III.

Memory is only necessary for those who insist upon novelty, I wrote on a small piece of paper as a note to myself some weeks ago, beginning to think about the danger of notebooks. Now I don't quite know what I meant. By memory I probably meant notebooks, documents kept in order to hold onto thoughts and experiences, documents intended to create an exomemory like an exoskeleton—notebooks as a shell to protect us from loss. I no longer know exactly what I meant by my epigram at the moment I was writing it to my future self; I have lost it in spite of itself. I imagine that it was an intense and provocative idea at the time, welding many loose stars into a single constellation. Otherwise I wouldn't have jotted it down. Also I must have believed I would know what I meant later. This is an interesting idea: Notes such as mine are actually promissory notes—when I write them to myself, I can enjoy the feeling that I have something wonderful to express, but I don't have to spell it out yet. The balloon payment lies far off in the future. This is a nice thing about notes, this promising feeling they give us with no work.

But for the purposes of stimulating or focusing thoughts, anything else works just as well as a note. All you really need is a little nick to the brain. Everyone has experienced this: When you are hungry, everything starts smelling good; when you have an idea, everything collaborates. In short, notes are no more

useful than the words on a matchbook—to the prepared mind. Because thinking wants only the tiniest
bit of novelty, the tiniest little bit of new per old. Our
novelty-obsessed culture disturbs the new-to-old ratio
in our minds and therefore makes it almost impossible to think. It is because people are so in the grip
of this novelty that they feel the desperate need to
keep notebooks against loss; they are convinced they
have so much to lose. If people were doing the same
thing over and over, rocked in the meditative arms of
repetition, they could have some real fun.

Real fun reminds me of the fun-loving British
poet Stevie Smith, who celebrated the novelty-free
life. Well, not quite novelty-free; it is a great pleasure to say no ("*Le Plaisir aristocratique de déplaire*")
though you must also occasionally say yes, "or you
will turn into an Oblomov. He stayed in bed all day
and was robbed by his servants. There was little enjoyment there." A great celebrator of the "regular habits"
which "sweeten simplicity," she says, "In the middle
of every morning I leave the kitchen and have a glass
of sherry with Aunt. I can only say that *this is glorious*." And because of her life of regular habits, the
rare interruption is almost hallucinogenic. She reports

seeing *The Trojan Women* on a friend's television. She is nearly undone with amusement at the hash it makes of Euripides: "What an earthshaking joke this is. Yet, if my life was not simple, if I looked at television all the time, I might have missed it."

Memory as a job, as a notebook to be kept, is only necessary for those who insist upon novelty. If you delight in habit as Stevie Smith did, if it is your pleasure to do things in the same way without inviting change, you don't have to write much down. And when things do change, as they will even without invitation, then you will really notice the change. Your memory will be deep, quiet, undifferentiated as a pool. Change will enter and twist like a drop of ink, the tiniest bit of new per old.

IV.

Remembering is not the negative of forgetting. Remembering is a form of forgetting. What a refreshing thing for Milan Kundera to say. He adds, "We can assiduously keep a diary and note every event. Rereading the entries one day, we will see that they cannot evoke a single concrete image." Yes. Like the photographs kept from childhood, our journals do not save but wipe away, or overlay, memory. It is so relaxing to think that we are an endless palimpsest, that the act of trying-to-keep is itself an act of erasure. It is so relaxing to give up the dream of getting back to Eden and to accept the smudges both on the paper and on our notebook-writing hand.

V.

Let me suggest a further extension of Kundera's law: Kundera says that remembering is a form of forgetting, but what if the reverse is also true, and *forgetting is a form of remembering*? This is a mysterious and lovely thought, that by letting our memories go they might somehow be returned to us. Here is "Forgetting," a short poem of mine which begins to nibble at this mystery:

Forgetting takes space.
Forgotten matters displace
as much anything else as
anything else. We must
skirt unlabeled crates
as though it made sense
and take them when we go
to other states.

In this poem we only know that what we have forgotten remains as an obstacle to be skirted and a burden to be hauled around. But this may only be the beginning of the truth. It could be that the very act of negotiating our way through a maze of unmarked boxes—the Etch-A-Sketch path of frustrating and apparently meaningless lefts and rights we're forced to take—is secretly correct; even, in some larger sense, efficient. If so, we need to show greater tolerance for our own apparent indirections. We may be living more fully than we know, in possession of every single thing that has ever happened to us and every thought we thought we forgot.

VI.

Here is "Forget What Did," a late poem from Larkin's *High Windows*. One of his dreary rock-versus-hard-place poems, it points up the difference between two sorts of diaries. Larkin has given up the habit of the first, the loss of which has left him stunned, and he can barely imagine the second.

Stopping the diary
Was a stun to memory,
Was a blank starting,

One no longer cicatrized
By such words, such actions
As bleakened waking.

I wanted them over,
Hurried to burial
And looked back on

Like the wars and winters
Missing behind the windows
Of an opaque childhood.

And the empty pages?
Should they ever be filled
Let it be with observed

Celestial recurrences,
The day the flowers come,
And when the birds go.

This is not one of Larkin's best poems. It is
too much under the sway of the diary he has stopped

keeping. He is afraid that in stopping the diary he has lost his memory, and this fear is making him dull. In his dullness he agrees to the insidious and common idea that whatever bad has happened in one's life is all there is to reality. His diary recorded the scarring words and actions (his? others'?) that "bleakened waking." Since he doesn't want to face this depressing pageant anymore, he stops the diary and therefore enters a "blank." The only undepressing diary he can possibly imagine is some sort of bland and blameless celestial timetable. It is a barren poem.

VII.

Tantalus, but without the curse.

Tantalus was a king who was cursed by the gods. What he desired receded as he approached. He was teased and tempted but he could never get anything into his mouth *because he was cursed.*

Many people think they live under a similar curse, which inhibits them from fully possessing their present or their past. They are maddened because when they try to reach for it, it draws away. But here is the secret: it's just how things are.

VIII.

I don't think I can speak at sufficient length about the importance to the poet of avoiding or ignoring Kodak moments. If a poet seeks to make or keep memories, how will she ever know which ones contain true power, which would assert themselves on their own? Perhaps her very definition of memory would change if she didn't get her Kodak moments developed. Maybe memory would not hold individual scenes at all; maybe it would have no detail; maybe it would not rise up—the pines of that morning in Yosemite scraping the interior of her skull; maybe it would be nacreous, layered regions of pleasure and attraction in the mind. Any sense of tint in the depth of the gleam would arise so slowly as to be imperceptible. I am speaking of the memory that might result from repetition. I am interested in the long ways of knowing, where the mind does not seek strangeness. We must be less in love with foreground if we want to see far.

IX.

When a dog first gets out of the water, he labors beneath the solid, heavy mass of his coat. But the dog knows to spraddle his four legs and violently agitate his body one way and then the other, producing a full-body halo of flung droplets and leaving his fur in alert spikes from shoulder to rump. He looks like a new beast—an in-between beast—not a drenched dog and not a dry dog. A porcudog or a hedgedog.

From Chihuahuas to Irish sheepdogs, all dogs know this maneuver. But we who walk on two legs do not find it so easy to shake off what weighs us down. We believe in the value of gravity: weight is worth. But we must shake weight off to write good poems. A poem, even if it comes up out of the darkest, saddest waters, will be a flung thing, a halo of prisms, the undoing, the dissolution of weight.

It may make some sort of shower. Larkin concludes his gorgeous poem "The Whitsun Weddings" with the image of an "arrow-shower." In this poem Larkin describes how he gradually realized that the repeated fusses at each local stop on his train journey to London were send-offs for newlyweds. He details the ordinariness of these couples and their well-wishers with such fascination that they grow vaguely grotesque. But gradually, gradually, the oppressive weight of these common couples with their commonplace futures becomes *rolling* weight, and not simply because they're on the train. Larkin's poem is itself a second train that becomes an engine of escape from the small plop ordinary lives make.

The poem glamours us with its "arrow-shower" ending. Here is Larkin, approaching that end but not there yet: As the train slows, nearing London, "it was nearly done, this frail / Travelling coincidence; and what it held / Stood ready to be loosed with all the power / That being changed can give." The beauty is that because this is *Larkin*, the reader must remain skeptical of the lyric flourish of "the power / That being changed can give." She cannot be sure yet that the idea of "being changed" isn't a trick; she must suspect that these young lumpen couples will soon find themselves less remarkably changed than they hoped and Larkin himself unglamoured—this "frail travelling coincidence" dispersed and proven no more than that. But then Larkin pulls a blessing out of his hat with a bit of pure, transported language. Or better, Larkin himself is pulled through the hat by a rapturous final image far beyond where intention can carry a poet: "And as the tightened brakes took hold, there swelled / A sense of falling, like an arrow-shower / Sent out of sight, some- where becoming rain." These lines give the reader the dazzling physical sensation of stopping and beginning *at once*, of seeing *beyond* seeing—one image transforming into the next—the slowing train and all its modest hopes mysteriously dissolving to a shower of arrows and the arrows falling as rain. We are catapulted out of the world of cautious, local coincidence into . . . into what? Glory.

This is the shake of a very great dog.

This poem is a porcudog bristling with details. Here details do not drag us down, do not persuade us that the dreariest gravity is the certainest truth; all the notebooks of detail are transformed.

So it isn't notebooks, or diaries, or spiral hinged objects as such that are ever the problem. It's getting stuck in them.

Do You Like It?

How a person becomes a poet is a mystery before which one must simply bow down. Perhaps one is born to it. Indeed, genetic preparations may have been underway for generations before the poet's birth. Snippings and mixings of hereditary materials may have been exactly calculated by some higher hand, one's hapless ancestors thrust together in otherwise unprofitable unions sheerly to produce the very poet one is. It could be that inevitable. It could be that grand and cruel. A person could be certifiably *called*, and of course this *is* an attractive theory, with religious overtones. It would be a ferocious religion, because so many generations would be used opportunistically, mined exclusively for their rhyme gene or their understanding of the caesura. But then, poetry *is* ferocious and opportunistic.

Or one may become a poet through an opposite process. Perhaps one is reduced to it. Instead of being the result of the refinement and purification of the blood

until only poetic ichor runs, the poet may be the product of some cataclysmic simplification, much like the
simplification that overtook the dinosaurs, wiping them
out and leaving the cockroaches. Both cockroach and
poet are hardy little survivors, quick and omnivorous.

But in any case, such speculations regarding the
origin of the poet feast upon the antique and the hideous
—always a pleasure, but quite unhelpful to the actual
poet in youth. For this is a fact: Though a person may
be absolutely destined to be a poet, the person doesn't
altogether understand this at first. For a long time the
person just feels silly.

It is very like the bewilderment felt by the early
evolutionary predecessor of the anglerfish, back before
this strange fish had undergone the "five hundred separate modifications" (Stephen Jay Gould's estimate) that
it took to develop the fishing lure it now dangles before
its cavernous mouth.

As in the case of this early anglerfish, the young
poet feels ill-formed, but with glimmers of something
yet to be articulated. This condition can go on throughout life, and, in truth, does. For how can the anglerfish
ancestor jump ahead to a more satisfying form where the
lure actually works? He cannot. And how can the poet

evolve beyond the comical, partial creature she is? She cannot. And still, she cannot live indefinitely without forming an opinion regarding immanence and glimmers.

I wonder if other poets can say how they became poets, not in terms of the imponderably remote sources of the gift or when they got a publishing break, but can they recall a particular moment when they felt themselves say yes to the lifelong enterprise? It always surprises me that I can name such a moment. I don't see myself as a person who has "moments." The circumstances were picturesque and dramatic in a way foreign to my desert-bred habits.

In 1976, at the age of thirty, I was bicycling across the United States. I had been feeling all the telltale symptoms of the poetic calling for a number of years, but was resisting it because I didn't like the part about being utterly exposed, inadequate, foolish, and doomed. Still, poetry kept commandeering my mind. So the bicycle trip was four thousand miles to say yes or no to poetry.

For a long time it didn't seem to be working.

Then came a morning, many hundreds of miles into the rhythm of riding, going up a long, high pass in the Colorado Rockies, when I felt my mind simply lose its edges. The pines swept through my mind, my mind swept through the pines, not a bit strange. All at once I no longer had to try to appreciate my experience or try to understand; I played with the phrase *the peace that passeth understanding* like turning a silver coin in my fingers. And with the peace-beyond-the-struggle-to-understand came an unprecedented freedom and power to think.

My brain was like a stunt kite; I held it by only a couple of strings, but I could ask anything, absolutely anything, of it. I tried some sample stunts, and then I asked the question: Shall I be a writer?

It was the one question of my whole life, but I asked it with no sense of weight, as though it were casual: Shall I be a writer?

I don't know where the answer came from, but it wasn't what I expected. I suppose I expected an evaluation of my talents and chances of success. What I heard was, *Do you like it?*

I had never heard anything so right. Yes; I did like it, that was all there was to it. I laughed and laughed and laughed.

II

The Authority
of Lightness

Like her poems, Stevie Smith is a cartoon from any distance at all. She takes very few strokes to draw and is refreshingly black, white, and flat. Both she and her poems are brilliant as singles, but also satisfy as strips. The strips needn't be read serially, however; they can be put in any order. This makes it hard for would-be critics of her verse and for biographers. But never mind. Jack Barbera and William McBrien, authors of *Stevie*, bravely march us through her life and works as though she progressed in the ordinary sense from birth to death and from juvenilia to resonant maturity of poetic voice. Occasionally she seems to oblige; the rest of the time she's the Ignatz of *Krazy Kat*, an appealing but untender fixed creature with a brick at the ready.

Stevie: A Biography of Stevie Smith, by Jack Barbera and William McBrien (Oxford University Press, 1987)

The few facts of her life are quickly dispatchable. Born in 1902, she spent all but her first four years in Palmers Green, since absorbed by London, in the company of a diminishing number of female relations boiling down finally to the exclusive company of her stern and noble "Lion Aunt." She worked as a secretary for many years until pensioned off for cutting her wrists in the office. She maintained a houseguest relationship to the ordinary run of life—the sexes coupled, children, pets—glad that she did not have to live there permanently (a sentiment shared by her hosts). She wrote three Shandyesque novels, a great deal of poetry accompanied by dashed-off drawings, short stories, radio broadcasts, plus many book reviews to supplement the pension. Her work was very much fancied by smart British people before World War II, then languished, then began to enjoy an international renaissance in the sixties, in time for her to relish it and become an eccentric star of the reading circuit and BBC. Her reputation is still on the rise, with *All the Poems* out from New Directions in 2016 and her authorized biography apparently in the works. She died in 1971 of a brain tumor, having, with her head shaved, finally taken on a dignified look, "rather like the death mask of John Donne," one friend noted.

Dignity, in any Thatcherly sense, was never her long suit. In fact, she eschewed long suits in general, having plumped early for some sort of short-skirted, schoolgirlish device that commentators shuddered at decade after decade. There was also that "fringe" she insisted upon, straight across the forehead. And the need for cosseting, waiting up well past her bedtime for her weekend hostess to fix her hot milk "as Aunt always did."

Going along with life is a great drain on one's resources. Because Stevie Smith got her tastes and behavior firmly fixed at an early age, she was left in possession of a great deal of energy that other people use up in adaptation. Smith always felt that it had particularly contributed to her independence of mind to have grown up in an all-female household. Most lower-middle-class women, she says in her third novel, *The Holiday*, are "conditioned early to having 'father' in the centre of home-life, with father's chair, and father's dinner, and father's *Times* and father says, so they are not brought up like me to be this wicked selfish creature." With a Lion Aunt always behind her she can safely be the "unicorn of fancy," unimpressed by all the father's chairs of social and literary opinion. Her poetry revels in this freedom from domination, creating wonderfully fanciful and fatherless rooms.

As first and last things, childhood and death, were always most interesting to Stevie Smith, so are they most interesting in her biography. She always recalls her Edwardian childhood as a "golden age." She loves her early schooling, getting the stirring rhymes that she never stopped loving (and abusing) by heart, building jungles in dress-boxes. And there is the delicious ritual of Anglican services. It is merely typical of Stevie Smith that she would decide in advance what hymn to sing of a Sunday, and sing it directly over the chorus of humble voices applied to the assigned text. Childhood provided her the purest pleasure in this kind of "doing otherwise." Even her early childhood stays in a TB sanitarium she found salutary for the preservation of the individual. She enjoyed the special treatment she received for being numbered among the sickest children, and she was able to begin refining her sense of alienation. By age eight she had acquired her own "flood subject." For Emily Dickinson it had been the thought of immortality; for Stevie Smith it was the cheering thought of suicide. Each poet finds such solace in her subject that she applies it like a hem to perhaps too many ragged sleeves. Nevertheless, these are indisputable sources of original power.

While always bucked up by Death, "the god who must come when you call," Stevie Smith managed to keep their relationship epistolary except on the one occasion in her fifty-first year. And then, though not released from life, she is released from her lifetime office job, which seems to be Death enough to keep her going until He comes on His own eighteen years later.

The middle chapters of the biography, devoted to Stevie Smith's "maturity," are the farrago of anecdote and commentary that seems difficult to avoid in documenting such a fixed character. These chapters can be enjoyed at random and, for an American reader especially, for their exquisite Britishness. It is sometimes difficult to sort out what in Stevie Smith is simply standard village-murder-mystery British and what is uniquely cockeyed, but either way, who will not relish Miss Smith laying on a guest lunch of *junket*, or another of boiled potatoes and a tin of peas? Or Miss Smith insisting upon rice pudding at the Piazza San Marco in Venice? (Our biographers conclude mildly that she was "certainly not Mediterranean-minded.") We can enjoy as well the lengthy consideration of whether or not Miss Smith ever "did the last fence," perhaps with George Orwell in a London park.

Love. This odd stickleback fish who bloats up and pokes would-be predators from the inside, what could she know about love? She was doubtful herself. She told a friend, shortly before her death, "When I am dead you must put people right. I loved my Aunt." And, because she kept herself "well on the edge" of it, she said, she loved life also. But of that middle human area between the pleasures of being cosseted and the pleasures of rain on a slate roof, she could know little. In "Dirge," one of her best-known poems, she says it for herself:

> From a friend's friend I taste friendship,
> From a friend's friend, love,
> My spirit in confusion,
> Long years I strove,
> But now I know that never
> Nearer I shall move,
> Than a friend's friend to friendship,
> To love than a friend's love.

There is great strength here. And perhaps great strength requires, or produces, a great distortion in its host. Still, the host is never sufficiently distorted to be free of the knowledge of her strangeness. She suffers not only the feelings appropriate to her nature, but also ghost feelings in the limbs she is born without. Stevie Smith is not one to obscure the hard truths about others (she was repeatedly threatened with libel) or about herself. She is deadly summary. She says what one might say if one were not dragged down by the very act of saying. She gives us poems in shapes that might result in a chamber free of the heart's gravity.

Stevie Smith knows she is locked in on the nursery side of the baby-viewing window, over there where life is new, cold, novel, alien, filled with competing cries, every baby an enemy. She is not strengthened by the instincts to nourish, protect, make room, compromise, couple, or step aside. She expresses the child's helplessness in a world it has not attached to but receives full-force. The child has the keenest sense of unequal powers, which would account for the fierceness and directness of her counterattacks.

But this is making it all sound much too dire. Stevie played with first and last things as one who grew up with wolves might play with wolves. She is lonely and hungry, and neither she nor the reader really wishes it otherwise. She always reminds us that she is doing it all from behind the privet hedge of Palmers Green: "Only those who have the luxury of a beautiful kindly bustling suburb that is theirs for the taking and of that 'customary domestic kindness' De Quincey speaks of, can indulge themselves in these antagonistic forest-thoughts," she confesses in a 1947 essay.

Stevie Smith never asks for your complicity in her feelings. In fact, she goes further: her whole poetic technique fairly drives you back. Hers are seldom the large generous sentiments to which each bosom returns an answer. Her poems offer different rewards. For one, the liberation from ourselves. A poem of Stevie Smith's does not become another thing which it is our responsibility to profit from. It is not "good" in that burdensome way whose secret subtext is that there is room for improvement in *you*. You are not required to improve each shining hour and you are not permitted to be empathetic.

A Stevie Smith poem has particular ways of defending itself from sympathetic ingestion. It keeps a tight rein over meaning, brooking no looseness of interpretation. It is about what it's about. It enforces rhyme patterns which are never allowed to appear subtle, natural, accidental, or musical beyond what an enthusiastic but amateur brass band might get up. The rhythms love to march off the parade route. It takes private delight in funny walks. It refuses to be round; it loves to go flat.

It goes exactly where most interested vision draws it. The reader is nobody's hypocrite brother. Your soul isn't compromised; it is simply threatened. Things are said briskly, uniformly briskly. It is a good technique to have if one is going to tell mortal truths. The comic sting of it in general takes away the sting of its burden—you are lonely, you are hungry, you are not understood. You are best so. You will die so. And through some paradox, this voice can achieve a rare tenderness, as it does in "Autumn":

> He told his life story to Mrs. Courtly
> Who was a widow. "Let us get married shortly,"
> He said. "I am no longer passionate,
> But we can have some conversation before it is
>   too late."

Stevie Smith is always going to spell trouble for anyone who feels it necessary to separate the joke from the deeper exercises of the heart. Even the Stevie-smitten Philip Larkin must end a prickly 1962 review of her poetry with the redemptive judgment that "Miss Smith's poems speak with the authority of sadness."

No doubt Miss Smith would counter that to speak at all is to confess sadness. She would hope that the authority comes from its brisk dispatch—the authority of lightness. Milan Kundera writes wistfully of the eponymous substance in *The Unbearable Lightness of Being*, describing how Beethoven once converted a perfectly inconsequential joke into a "serious quartet." He contemplates how much more remarkable it would have been if Beethoven had achieved the reverse, making "heavy go to light." He says with real pain that we don't know how to think this way. But if, for a moment, we could give up the prejudices of gravity, which most values that which is most obedient to its force, if we could read her in space, we would find in Stevie Smith a most unencumbering soul. We tend to think either that poetry is superior entertainment or that poetry approaches higher truths. But what if higher truths are really entertaining: what if the ultimate forms are ravishing cartoons?

Here is Stevie Smith on the subject of poetry in "My Muse," from the excellent *Me Again*, uncollected writings of Stevie Smith edited by our biographers back in 1982 and attesting to their enduring interest in their subject. After saying that poetry is fierce, absolute, dangerous, not neat, without kindness at all, "the strong way out," she says: "All the poems Poetry writes may be called,

'Heaven, a Detail,' or 'Hell, a Detail.'" She likens Poetry to "the goddess Thetis who turned herself into a crab with silver feet, that Peleus sought for and held. Then in his hands she became first a fire, then a serpent, then a suffocating stench. But Peleus put sand on his hands and wrapped his body in sodden sacking and so held her through all her changes, till she became Thetis again, and so he married her, and an unhappy marriage it was."

Note the characteristic Stevie Smith tag. She concocts this great polymorphic struggle only to reduce it in her British saucepot to a Palmers Green domestic mismatch. She will simply not be rattled by grandeur. Exalted and terrible moments will occur. "Riding home one night late on a bus," she writes in another essay, "I was lost forever in the swirling streets of that reflected world, with its panic corners and the distances that end too soon; lost and never to come home again." But what one emphasizes above them, below them, through them, is order.

At age sixty-two, she writes in a characteristically short essay, "Simply Living": "I enjoy myself now living simply. I look after somebody who used to look after me." She likes to spend time in the kitchen: "I like food, I like stripping vegetables of their skins, I

like to have a slim young parsnip under my knife."
(A pity she didn't serve them to guests.) Then there is
the morning glass of sherry with Aunt: "I can only say
that *this is glorious*." What puts the edge on the routine
are those "moments of despair that come sometimes,
when night sets in and a white fog presses against the
windows. Then our house changes its shape, rears up
and becomes a place of despair. Then fear and rage run
simply—and the thought of Death as a friend."

Whatever strong conclusion one of her poems may
draw, the next is likely to run the other way. On one page
there is the admonition to carry on; on the opposite there
is the yearning for escape through death or war work.
She is never out of the crisscross storms no matter how
safely she tucks herself in with Aunt. Still Stevie Smith
is no existential hero, bravely bearing the irreconcilable
ambiguities. They are not to be borne. They are to be
fried in the frying pan, caught in mousetraps, dipped
in paint-cans, and marched off planks with the gusto
of Tom and Jerry's battles. It is as though poetry really
were, as Eliot claimed, superior amusement.

Stevie Smith's Miss Snooks, Mrs. Osmosis ("all
right in small doses"), Lord Mopes, jungle husbands,
swinging apes, singing cats, voices of God and other

primary movers, dogs, knights, and frogs go beyond
Emily Dickinson's directive to tell it slant. They tell it
in Sunday-school felt-board figures. Yet she insists that
her poetry is the best and most of her: "Everything I
have lived through, and done, and seen, and read and
imagined and thought and argued." She gives her life
to her cut-outs and caricatures because it "gives proportion and eases the pressure, puts the feelings at one
remove, cools the fever."

Stevie Smith does everything possible to cartoonify
herself and her work. She is perfectly capable of saying
onstage that much of her poetry "may be understood as a
soft sighing after shadowy death." But this does nothing
to prevent the cartoon from being grand. Stevie Smith's
poems, so doggerelish, so faux faux, so clearly enjoying themselves in their headstrong way, so thoroughly
"unnatural," can't in the long run be separated from the
True, the Beautiful, the Timeless, the deeply moving.
It is terrible in a way that there is not one language for
the Truth and another for the Joke but there is not. Arti-
fice will groan like a common trestle under our grief.
Anything can do anything. A clumsily rhymed retell-
ing of the fairy tale "The Frog Prince," illustrated with
a drawing of a heavy-lidded toad apparently suffering

with a stomachache, can weigh up the mortal cost of enchantment and remain weightless itself.

But let us return to Palmers Green. The Lion Aunt survives upstairs in her dignity until the age of ninety-six, leaving Stevie Smith only three years to live out alone in the house on Avondale Road. Her sister has a stroke and Smith's own health deteriorates in these final years, but the Stevie spirit is if anything refined by tribulation. After her aunt's death she writes a poem about how we must not refuse suffering, "So to fatness come." It has the always-obvious Stevie Smith rhymes hiccoughing down the ragged right side, and it twists syntax to get them; it has the archaic "thy's" and "spakes"; it is no less than the voice of Grief addressed to the whole of the "Poor human race." It features not just the "dish" of pain but the "cup" of it as well. (One suspects that this additional vessel appears because she wanted to do something later with the words "sup" and "up.") The last stanza abandons all attempt at rhyme. The authorial I comes in and says that the preceding address by Grief occurred to her in a dream, and concludes with Johnsonian dignity: "I thought / He spoke no more than grace allowed / And no less than truth." And what is the effect of this mix? It is grand, restrained, glowing with probity, inevitable, ancient, biblical, immediate, fresh, and unencumbering.

The Stevie Method of Life and Poetry turns out to work very well, despite her lifetime caveats. Call her childlike, or childish; say that it is unattractive for a grown woman to steal the good stuff out of the tea sandwiches; but add that her method of getting along was sustainable, that her solitary stand, her combination of fierceness and indecision, her tweaking of demons' beaks, continued to nourish as well as any of the more familiar modes. It was, the evidence suggests, neither too brittle nor too heavy to go on serving. She may craze and crack, but she never comes down of her own weight like the Roman Empire. And here is the cheerful news for the outsider, the one among us who is never caught behind the knees by the chairlift of Life: the outsider can get along in a way that isn't tragic, that continues brave and enlivening.

Even the brain tumor that kills her seems a final Stevie joke. She had always praised tiredness for its tendency to shift words "a bit offbeam," turning a word like *lodestar* into *lobster*, for instance, and engendering the wonderfully silly poem "Duty Was His Lodestar," beginning "Duty was my Lobster, my Lobster was she, / And when I walked with my Lobster / I was happy." And now the tumor pressing on her brain accelerates the gift. The images in her last letters, published in *Stevie* and also in *Me Again*, are like ammunition going off in a burning house. It's an end which Stevie Smith would have enjoyed, given greater distance.

Inedible Melons

Marianne Moore's poems are as contemporary as a Google search and as antique as wonder cabinets. Her method for going forward in a poem is so barnacled and elaborate that one might question whether she goes forward or not. She really has very little interest in forward drive—perhaps progress smacked to her of base qualities such as striving or pugnacity. Nevertheless, she arranges to at least simulate the sensation of forward motion through linking object to object in her wonder cabinets. The poems are glass-cased and filled with small sliding drawers which we open. Our fascination with any part both blinds us to the rest (and to the fact that the connections may be casual) and convinces us that the whole *would*, by extrapolation, be more than the sum of its priceless parts if we could ever apprehend it, which we *cannot*. This is not a criticism but

The Poems of Marianne Moore, ed. Grace Schulman (Viking, 2003)

an observation. The reader can go from part to part, relishing detail and secure in the powerful sense that Marianne Moore is somehow taking care of the big picture. She has taken as her subject matter that which she has found in museums, books, and zoos, but the power of her voice and her moral presence assure us that her understanding is not intermittent but constant, and that we may—we should—abandon ourselves to the study of wonders, confident that Miss Moore could—and probably will—handle the dragon attacks.

What a desirable presence. Marianne Moore was this curio—who was so much more, who really did seem to hold steady and brave. She strikes me as at once ridiculous and immensely cheering. She is monumental, like a stern aunt, and all bits and pieces, like a pixilated one.

To return to the question of progress in her poems and why it was a bit of a bother to her, Marianne Moore really was working to an end other than "getting someplace." Her object was the liberation of the mind, and she felt that exactness of description was the great liberator. When interviewed by Donald Hall for the *Paris Review*, she praised the methods of scientific inquiry, saying, "Precision, economy of statement, logic employed to ends that are disinterested, drawing and identifying, liberate—at least have some bearing on—the imagination." And these are the golden virtues of Miss Moore's own "product" (the scientific-sounding term she characteristically applied to her own poems). She aims to liberate the mind. It is an elegant paradox that close application to the physical somehow does release the mind from the physical. There is probably never a time when poetry couldn't stand a good dose of Marianne Moore's profound respect for the mind and her tonic view of the poet's job. She will always represent a grease-cutting alternative to the poetry of self-occupation.

Marianne Moore is the opposite of sticky; she is constitutionally fearless, cheerful, and cool. She aspires to disinterestedness. She is not dissecting or mending the heart. She is trying out formal possibilities, and calls her "product" "observations, experiments in rhythm, or exercises in composition." She says to Hall about attending bohemian parties in New York unchaperoned that "I felt impervious," and this could be applied to her attitude to life in general. Her vulnerability—artistically—was internal, that is, her struggle with her own interior conflict, which, happily for us, she couldn't resolve.

Not that she harps on conflict as the source of poetry. She is not one of the aggressively suffering poets.

Her impulse to write, she says, is that she is "charmed" by
something. She begins with "a felicitous phrase . . . simul-
taneous usually with some thought or object of equal
attraction: 'Its leaps should be *set* / to the flageo*let*.'" In
other words, two different things are brought together—
with rhyme often advancing the second, as it does in her
illustration. It's such a lovely, untormented beginning.
The abiding torment—or at least chronic aggravation—
comes from what sounds like a technical problem but is
in fact a tectonic one. She puts it this way: "The most
difficult thing for me is to be satisfactorily lucid, yet
have enough implication . . . to suit myself. . . . I do not
approve of my 'enigmas,' or as somebody said, 'the not
un-green grass.'" She cannot resolve this, and will not
resolve it falsely. These two impulses grind at each other
like the plates of the earth, however one might think a
poet's great struggle should sound a little meatier.

  Marianne Moore cannot put ideas together for us,
in her poetry or her essays. There's no point asking. She's
not following the Modernist fashion of her time; she just
can't, in all conscience, put things together. This may
be the very quality that makes her particularly irresistible to the excessively smart and educated. She refuses
what scholars often find difficult to refuse, which is to

accumulate and become large and ovoid. She is even better than Humpty Dumpty, whom we love because he *crashed*. For Marianne Moore it is an heroic crash—an acknowledgment that the processes of the mind do not roll on like a steamroller but operate by reversals and leaps, and that one must steadfastly withstand society's tiresome insistence that one maintain a continuous shell.

Marianne Moore's poems break up; that's all there is to it. One treasures incomparable lines: the mussel, "opening and shutting itself like an injured fan"; the student, "too reclusive for / some things to seem to touch / him, not because he / has no feeling but because he has too much." Is that a problem? Don't we generally do that with poems we love, recall a phrase, or a line or two, exactly, nestled inside some vaguer rhythmic texture? It's the best I can usually do. When, for example, I repeat to myself Frost's "and to do that to birds was why she came," the pang I feel depends upon the thirteen lines I can't remember. I know that this final line is somehow the product of the previous thirteen, and by remembering the sum, I am remembering the equation. Of course, remembering lines from Marianne Moore is different because her poems do not move forward or build in the way Frost's do. Great lines in a Marianne Moore poem aren't exactly *results*. They are more like particles in suspension. They depend upon whatever is holding them in place, but it's more the way jewels need the prongs of the setting.

Emotion is shifty, unstable stuff for Marianne Moore. Strong emotion tolerates the use of generalization; being accurate defuses the emotion, mastering it through dispersion. In speaking years later of her much-celebrated anti-war poem, "In Distrust of Merits," she cannot approve of her work: "emotion overpowered me." She finds it "haphazard; . . . disjointed, exclamatory." She distrusts and is embarrassed by too direct or coarse an expression of feelings—but she isn't embarrassed to be embarrassed. In fact, embarrassment shows up as a badge of distinction as early as her previously unpublished poem "We All Know It," undated, but written before she was twenty-four. After first deferring to what we "all know," which is that "silence is best" (a point she often revisits over the years), she sets about opening up a little beachhead for art and the artist: "the realm of art is the realm in / Which to look for 'fishbones in the throat of the gang.' Pin / Pricks and the unstereotyped embarrassment being the contin / Ual diet of artists." Within the difficult locutions and the splittings of words for the sake of rhyme is something quite wonderful—that "unstereotyped embarrassment" which she says is part of the artist's prickly diet. This is not regular embarrassment, but the artist's unique varietal. In the case of the poet, I would suspect that the embarrassment might result partly from exposure to conventional (stereotyped, generalized) expressions of feelings or thoughts by the "gang," an allergic reaction to boilerplate. And for a sensibility such as Marianne Moore's, pretty much everything is boilerplate. The embarrassment would arise too from the poet's own inability to express her feelings as exactly as the object of her feelings deserves. From the get-go she is bridling at the thought of saying anything directly, and bridling at being criticized for saying things too indirectly. This poem ends with an amusingly clear declaration of what she thinks about clear declarations: "It is / A strange idea that one must say what one thinks in order to be understood." Perhaps beneath these strata of embarrassment is the embarrassment of having feelings at all. It is embarrassing to be human, and of course Marianne Moore frequently slips into the form of some better-protected animal, less porous and translucent. Embarrassment at being human may be a deeper provocation to artistic production than we usually think.

I am beginning to think of this lifelong inner debate (in which she regularly assumes both voices— the voice that says, "You *must* say it straight" and the voice which counters, "It can't be said any straighter than I just said it") as a kind of lover's quarrel that compels and repels, as odd as that sounds. There is something so intimate, irresolvable, and inescapable about the two-party battle, with a lover's subtle feints and parries, gallantries and insistence. I don't quite know what to call it. I might just as easily consider it temporizing. Consider: Marianne Moore is embarrassed by—betrayed by—feelings. So what will she do? She will describe the world of plants, animals, and things up close; she will dissect human behavior from a distance. And, above all, she will do what we all do when we don't want to eat something we are required to eat: *she will move things around on her plate.* Whatever the case, her poems wind up strangely electrified with the feelings she will not directly countenance.

In having recently read a great deal of Marianne Moore's work, I have come to a surprising, not quite mental but not exclusively muscular, sensation: the extravagantly gorgeous linguistically tormented lacuna-pocked poems of Marianne Moore are *simple* in some essential way, and *relaxing* to read. (I see a note to myself, on a page about a third of the way into the book, that says, "I am starting to understand much more—as I give up.") The difficulties seem to me now on the surface and not hidden underneath. If you read enough of her you begin to see what occupies her, and has occupied her from youth.

Marianne Moore must teach us to read her. Her poems are instructions in how to read her poems. She must polish us until we are bright enough to see her; she must refine our ability to discriminate before we can apprehend her discriminations. Marianne Moore has said, "originality is the byproduct of sincerity," a pronouncement worthy of savoring for its economy alone, and worthier still as a key to understanding her simplicity. All those high jinks, all those arabesques of argument and expression, all those exact and exacting quotations that are characteristic of Marianne Moore's poetry are utterly sincere; and a certain rest is afforded by this deep and incontestable sincerity. She is saying it as straight as she can, and that fact preserves her beautiful house of cards (mostly face cards, of course, seventeenth-century French). The winds of impatience do blow, but they don't blow her down.

Which is not to say the reader is not impatient. *Never* will one's tools be fine enough to pick her locks. I want simultaneously to memorize her and throw her down. There is something repellent in all this. But I am convinced that for a poet to be great we must find ourselves repelled by some part of the poet's work. Not just mildly disquieted, but actively repelled. So Marianne Moore is repulsive, extreme, in her scrupulosity. (The great critic Randall Jarrell, in trying to describe what about Marianne Moore's poetry put readers off, listed "her extraordinary discrimination, precision and restraint, the odd propriety of her imagination." He adored her work, by the way.) There has got to be a fanaticism—it doesn't matter, it can be the fanaticism of fastidiousness—but there has to be some private path the reader just can't follow all the way. There must be a crack in the poet of some sort. It has to be deep, privately potent, and unmendable—and the poet must forever try to mend it.

The primary satisfaction of reading the early unpublished poems is not the chips of greatness in them, but the satisfaction of putting to rest once and for all any thought that Marianne Moore was ever any different. Here she is at eight:

Dear St. Nicklus;

This Christmas morn
You do adorn
Bring Warner a horn
And me a doll
That is all.

One notes that she has made the title (including punctuation) a part of her poem, a habit she'd keep. One might add that she displays her lifelong good manners in requesting something for her beloved older brother, Warner, before asking for something for herself. We further note that the poem delights in rhyme and appropriates the ten-dollar word "adorn"—which doesn't quite fit—to serve it. But it is perhaps the extratextual fact that her mother saved this scrap (originally illustrated, apparently) that augers most about Marianne Moore's future, since her mother would remain so intimately involved in her writing.

It's fun to look back at a great poet's juvenilia—clotted, arch, whatever. Every young writer has parts that don't fit together; you see Marianne Moore trying this tack and that, getting one effect at the complete expense of the other, then the other at the expense of the first. What distinguishes the poet who continues to write, and who develops a genuinely distinctive voice, is her inability to sacrifice the incompatible parts, her interior requirement to have it all and to forge some way with words in order to get it all. This is a tall and weird order. She must not only bring together all that is essential to her, she must leave out everything that isn't right for her. And it may be that what isn't right for her *is* right for most people. As a result, her work will look odd, not only—or perhaps not primarily—because of what she must put in, but because of what she must leave out. In Marianne Moore's case she had to leave out things like connectors between ideas—which she privately disdained as "padding"—and she had to leave out life. This latter is a paradoxical thing to say, because who in the world was ever more alive in her writing. Her observations are so famously keen that they cut or freeze or burn, physical in their vigor. But we also know that something is missing, in the ordinary sense.

Right away Marianne Moore is worrying her something missing. In the early poems from 1907 to 1913—she'd be twenty to twenty-six—she introduces the "don't touch" theme. Here is an example:

A Red Flower

Emotion,
Cast upon the pot,
Will make it
Overflow, or not,
According
As you can refrain
From fingering
The leaves again.

Clearly, despite the strangeness of imagining emotion as Miracle-Gro, a little feeling goes a long way. And look at this:

A Fish

No heart was planted in my body.
God knows how that came to be.
But in vouchsafing me that loss, He
Has vouchsafed me courtesy.

She is looking around inside herself and she is finding herself a fish, don't you think? That is a brave thing to do. And she's not miserable about it; it has its compensatory "courtesy." Miss Moore became known for her mandarin displays of courtesy. Courtesy eventually looms so large for Miss Moore that it is a sort of warrior's path. When in later life she admires La Fontaine's "surgical kind of courtesy" she is also admiring her own. (She is a great admirer of "qualities" and in this courteous way she is able to defend her own qualities.) Her warrior's tools are what? Admiration? Courtesy? Oh, it's too much fun to find links between the early and the later Moore. From the start, she dwells on unapproachable animals, she describes beautiful objects, she defends art as "exact perception," she inveighs against flattery and falseness, she exalts virtues—courage, modesty, economy, flintiness, keeping one's distance—she demonstrates staunch Presbyterian upstandingness and faith, and extols the good sort of mulishness: the mule's skepticism, sure-footedness, and kick. In terms of form, she experiments flamboyantly, her lines jagging across the page or forming shapes. She rhymes extravagantly or is extravagantly prosy, and those trademark quotations also begin peppering her work. Plus I must add that we endure a lot of high-sounding inscrutability. I can't help quoting all of the following poem:

Reprobate Silver

Freighted with allusion "of the sort to which we are
    accustomed,"
Hand wrought slang—in the spirit of Cellini and
    after the manner of Thor—

Like Panshin's horse, not permitted to be willful,
Trembling incessantly and champing at the bit—
It is worthy of examination.
It is quite as much a matter of art as the careful
And a kind of Carthage by Flaubert.
It is like the castles in the air that manufacture
    themselves

Out of clouds before our eyes
When we are listening to a scientific explanation of
    things in which we are

                                    not interested.
The fact that there is no justification for its existence
And that perhaps it had to be written
About what ought never to have been written at all.

When a poet delights us, it's amazing how much
we'll put up with. I feel as indulgent and proud as a par-
ent. First consider the hilarious incompatibility of the title

words, "Reprobate Silver." What a perfect description of
MM. Is she not criminally polished? (That's the problem
with writing about Marianne Moore; she has already
said everything about herself, and said it *better*.) Then
listen to her name-drop (Cellini, Thor, Panshin—who
is Panshin, anyhow?—Flaubert). See the cavalier bold-
ness of her segues, hear the grand thump of those final
imponderables landing in one's lap like inedible melons.
Some of the incoherencies in the poem are so odd that
one thinks perhaps parts of her original are missing.
But what I really want to say is that a bit of something
essential and dazzling comes tearing through this screen.
When she writes "Like Panshin's horse, not permitted to
be willful, / trembling incessantly and champing at the
bit," she has managed a fine compression. The horse itself
contains compressed opposites: it obeys, but it trembles
and champs, its willfulness expressed only in nerves. One
immediately imagines this high-strung thoroughbred,
a picture of barely reined in energy (and beauty) that is
thrilling on its own. She employs this horse first as an
analogy to the spirit of the metalsmith who one supposes
created some reprobate silver thing she is contemplating,
and beyond that to suggest the contained energy in the
silver thing itself, giving us three levels of horse so far.

But one does not care as much about these applications as about the application of the horse image to Miss Moore herself, for this is a self-portrait. She is the trembling horse "not permitted to be willful." And of course she is also the one who prevents the horse from being willful. And then, because it is a very good self-portrait, its application is universal; we each know this feeling that she has described in not describing any feelings. Somehow this Rube Goldbergian contraption of a poem is also the alchemist's flame in which we see the fiery, and checked, spirit of Marianne Moore.

I don't imagine I could have stood the convolutions of this poem if I weren't reading backwards, with knowledge of her mature work. But by now she's trained me to find her. She latches and thrives upon the tension between freedom and restraint. It is the wellspring of so many fruitful conflicts in her poems. And it really is another form of the tension she maintains between complexity and clarity. In one of these early poems, she asserts, "Mixed metaphors are not necessarily," thus plumping for complexity. Yet in the next poem she can be perfectly mulish in her resistance to her own thoroughbred instincts. (An early poem is titled, in quotations, "'I Like a Horse but I Have a Fellow

Feeling for a Mule.'") She will neither give up to her endlessly competing discriminations nor give them up.

Marianne Moore's reputation is burdened with a primness and overrefinement that are the hazard of living all one's life with one's mother and performing further surgery on split hairs, but she absolutely loved to kick. What she said of William Carlos Williams's poetry is true of hers as well: "He is willing to be reckless; if you can't be that, what's the point of the whole thing?" She was also willing to cast a cold eye. In "Old Tiger," one of the best of the poems that have never before been collected, she celebrates the tiger as a remote, disdainful observer, with a "fixed, abstracted lizardlike expression of / the eye which is characteristic of all accurate observers." She relishes the tiger's adamance and ferocity: "you to whom a no / is never a no, loving to succeed where all others have failed, so / constituted that opposition is pastime and struggle is meat." Perhaps she is not as goaded as a tiger but she is goaded enough: "you see more than I see but even I / see too much."

There is something so odd about her technique. She commonly looks at something quite remote and static, such as a piece of silver or an illustration—it is an illustration that lies behind "Old Tiger," for example—and it explodes in a variety of alarming directions. She is praised endlessly, and rightly, for the unparalleled fineness of her observation. Here, to offer a nearly random example, is the chimpanzee the old tiger is looking at: "An exemplary hind leg hanging like a plummet at the end of a / string—the tufts of fur depressed like grass on which something heavy has been lying." Yet in another way observation is just the detonator for an explosion of private associations, glittering in their rhetorical arcs, and upon their descent into the reader's brainpan randomly meaningful and meaningless. At the end of this poem, when she announces triumphantly to the tiger, "you / know that it is not necessary to live in order to be alive," I feel like applauding, but I am not sure why. I have spent some time trying to put the pieces of this poem together. I feel sure that it is a triumph, but it's like trying to pack a suitcase in dreams. If I get one piece, I lose another.

Marianne Moore despises the pious assumption that simplicity equals truth and excoriates the simplifiers. Here she condemns the poor devil George Moore, who on some occasion apparently took too much out of a story: "Your soul's supplanter, / the spirit of good narrative, flatters you, convinced that in reporting briefly /

One choice incident, you have known beauty other than of [pig]stys." And here she casts the "Pedantic Literalist" (a pair of words that combine everything she loathes) down into the fake-palm-tree ring of hell: "What stood / erect in you has withered. A / little 'palm-tree of turned wood' / informs your once spontaneous core." I always have a double feeling, reading lines like these. Oh, more than double. I love to see her spank the lightweights, the pedants, the intellectual posers; I love the pure eccentricity of her language; and I think, *who will ever read this?* A poet friend of mine recently said, "They should have taken away her library card." God, it's true; she goes on and on. I can barely hold onto a single whole poem. And at the same time I think she is the Statue of Liberty.

In "The Ardent Platonist" she writes, "to understand / One is not to find one formidable." She's right; if one is formidable, one is not understood. But how can we not find Marianne Moore formidable since she's so hard to understand? I think we just have to read her until we can contain the complexity that we cannot resolve. That is a bigger kind of understanding. At that point, the poet is no longer "formidable." A word or two becomes sufficient to invoke the complex spirit. We feel, now, an affection, a human affection, and a receptiveness which we could not feel when we were fighting with particulars. But maybe I'm just preaching to myself here, since I am irksomely literal when I read poetry (having a small palm tree where my core should be).

In her beautiful poem "In the Days of Prismatic Color," her treatment of complexity is for once sufficiently linear so that the ball she hits is actually the same ball that sails out of the park. She powers through the whole question before complexity gets a chance to ruin the game by throwing in extra balls. She begins her poem by considering "obliqueness." Originally, in Adam's time, "obliqueness was a variation / of the perpendicular, plain to see and / to account for." That is so funny and cartoonlike, an early geometry diagram: oblique doesn't mean hard to understand; it simply means not perpendicular—a reading that goes nicely with her love of the briskly scientific. However, this brief paradise doesn't even survive Eve's arrival; it was only "when Adam was alone." So for a very long time we have been in the grip of postlapsarian obliqueness, which she equates with "complexity." Of complexity, there are two types: first, the complexity "committed to darkness" which "instead of granting itself to be the pestilence that it is, moves all a / bout as if to bewilder us with the dismal

/ fallacy that insistence / is the measure of achievement and that all truth must be dark." This is the complexity that passes itself off as "sophistication." And it is "at the antipodes of the init / ial great truths." The second type of complexity contains the great truths, and its lineaments are a spectacular mess; "'Part of it was crawling, part of it / was about to crawl, the rest / was torpid in its lair.'" Truth *is* messy—but it is enduring: "Truth is no Apollo / Belvedere, no formal thing. The wave may go over it if it likes. / Know that it will be there when it says, / 'I shall be there when the wave goes by.'" What better or more beautiful argument could be made for the endurance of Marianne Moore's poetry, which despises all the ways that complexity can be used to obscure and celebrates all that give us another angle from which to see and survive? If Marianne Moore were a tomato farmer today, she'd be planting the fantastic bulging and lobed heritage varieties that shape themselves to their difficult soils. She is the champion of multiplicity because it is the only principle that guarantees survival. She has said, "It is a privilege to see so much confusion."

The tension of intellectual argument is the source of energy in her poems. She presses repelling magnets toward each other inside the contained space of the poem, and argument slips and slides. Her surrogates try to flip each other over in this strange land of repulsion. She is fearless in the pursuit of her argument, leaping from shape to shape at its requirement, as single-minded as a superhero chasing a villain across New York rooftops. And that's the interesting thing: behind the chronic shape-shifting, the drifting continents of coherence, one simply never doubts that there is a steady, utterly principled vision; every time I read her I am shocked anew at how forceful and dominating her voice is. She loves the prose of Dr. Johnson, and her strange arguments achieve that same towering probity. She can vacillate as often as she wants (she was forever revising her poems, over the course of decades); she can deny that she has a steady center, or "tap root"; she can plead whispiness ("I am so naive, so docile" with such an "ardor to be helped")—but her particles are so very fond of each other that they simply jump together in our mind, wherever they are in her poems. I am tempted to believe that there is a Marianne Moore over-poem that we are reading.

Yes, certainly we are reading a Marianne Moore over-poem, as we are for every poet we love enough to know well, or know well enough to love. Today, reading a posthumous Philip Larkin poem in the *New*

Yorker, I felt this over-thing so sharply. There was Larkin's voice again, so welcome. His lovely poem wasn't alone, stranded on the page, to be read in isolation. In me it had someone who knew its family. Or maybe I *was* its family, if we admit the possibility that we are really not individuals who read poems and make them our own, but rather that poems make us their own, that we are a poem-delivery system, or poem clearinghouse, allowing the poems of the immortals to reunite with their families—a new Larkin is embraced (morosely) by the Larkins, a Moore (courteously) by the Moores. It felt this personal, and impersonal.

The Poems of Marianne Moore fills a real need. It does not claim to be "complete"—there are only a handful of her translations of *The Fables of La Fontaine* for example. But it could hardly be complete what with Marianne Moore's lifetime of scissorings and pastings which sometimes resulted in as many as a half dozen different published versions. What we do get is all of her clanking but revealing juvenilia and a number of other never-collected poems, totaling more than a hundred new ones. The organization is chronological, which makes good sense in every way except the way in which it scrambles Marianne Moore's own famously unhelpful notes to her poems. These still follow the organization of her earlier collections and are thus hard to match up. But this is small potatoes next to Grace Schulman's heroic accomplishment, not just in uncovering so many lost poems, but in restoring favorite poems to their favorite unshrunk size while retaining Moore's snipped variants in the generous and scholarly Editor's Notes. What a task it must have been to get this refracting crystal palace of work assembled without benefit of instructions, and how beautifully and unpedantically Grace Schulman has accomplished it. Her introduction is short, insightful, and warmly personal, profiting from her friendship with Marianne Moore beginning when Schulman was fourteen and continuing until Moore's death in 1972.

A virtue of poetry is that a little goes a long way, and Marianne Moore's poetry is especially virtuous. We could probably find her in a grain of Moore sand, once we're a bit trained, but that isn't the thing. We will probably add few new favorites to our favorites list, and that isn't the thing. The thing is, all her poems are at last in one place, as they should be.

Fidget and Gnash

"The handkerchiefs almost frighten us by their perfection." Who but Marianne Moore could possibly have written this? Her *Selected Letters* (Alfred A. Knopf, 1997) offers up a ridiculous sublimity of letter-writing in which nothing, not the least gift of handkerchiefs, escapes meticulous apostrophe. We are not just talking precision of expression here; we are talking the very torments of rapture and the characteristic strain they put on the fabric of Moore's sentences: "Even a bungler must see that maintained rectangles in drawn-work so tenuous and complicated, required genius and many years' apprenticeship; and the fineness of the material is to begin with a constant wonder." Everything all the way around the unassailable fact of Marianne Moore's genius strikes one as slightly, well, slightly *comical*. We bounce off a truly original mind like rubber balls. Even

The Selected Letters of Marianne Moore, ed. Bonnie Costello (Knopf, 1997)

Elizabeth Bishop, in "Efforts of Affection," the beautiful memoir of her mentor, is deflected from the central mystery of such a person. Bishop can only gesture
toward "the rarity of true originality and the sort of
alienation it might involve" and then turn back to the
pleasures of anecdote. It is hard not to limn Moore as an
endearing character, a precious curio. But of course this
is the paradox of Marianne Moore. In a sense her poems,
also, are precious curios—which seems like the wrong
thing to say about achievements so great and enduring.
Marianne Moore compels us to a special discomfort:
she represents a sort of sustained impossibility; we are
bounced between awe and amusement.

Moore's letters reveal how literal her poems are,
how of a piece with her life. Everywhere is evidence
of her darting, delicate, exacting, pan-interested mind.
Detail is poetry to her. Throughout her life she receives
exotic bric-a-brac from traveling friends. Her exquisite
appreciations stimulate further gifts, and the cycle continues, object to object, pleasure irresistibly inviting pleasure, leapfrogging like her poems. She writes to Elizabeth
Bishop, "It may be a mistake to pore over minutiae as I
do but it makes such work as the carved capitals on the
cards of the Madeleine, an active poem." Nothing that

is New York is alien to her—she loves the zoo, naturally, and the Natural History Museum, and all the other museums, but she also loves the ill-attended lecture by an authority on pears, and the rodeo at Madison Square Garden where "one contestant wore carmine goat's fur chaps with tufts of black goat's fur inserted at regular intervals, on the principle of kings' ermine."

It takes a deep security to endure a life of such endless lightness, tangled delicacy, nearly mad fealty to serial perfections, almost comic probity. Less secure people have to be denser and more flat-footed. The letters help us see what made her so strong. Above all there was her family, which was nearly one creature. It was a small family, her awesome mother with whom she lived until Mrs. Moore died when Marianne was fifty-nine, and her navy chaplain brother, Warner. Moore's many family letters reveal the sort of furry burrow-dwellers' tumbling intimacy that the three enjoyed. They had endless animal names for one another—Badger, Bear, Mole, Fangs, Ratty—and these names shifted loosely among them. Marianne was always referred to as "he," both in her mother's letters to Warner and in her own. She sometimes signed herself "your brother." Moore never seemed to pine for other company; she reports up to "7 suitors" at one time in youth, but they seem to have done little more than make her "fidget and gnash." She enjoys an obvious satisfaction in the great lifelong "we" of herself and her mother in the small Brooklyn apartment they shared, the two of them maintaining the highest standards of grammar, wit, and moral character; attending poetry readings and animal movies; remaking not only the dresses and coats that Marianne's rich friends were always passing along but also Moore's poems, which had to pass "under the maternal clippers"—and all the while having the full roster of modernist poetry over for simple lunches and complex conversation. "I am cautious . . . about encouraging visitors who . . . might bore my mother. She is over the heads of most of them," confesses Moore to old friend Ezra Pound.

In addition to the security her family provided her, Moore simply seemed to be born emotionally unhandicapped and at ease with her own nature. When the poet Bryher wants to give Moore money in the 1920s to release her from her part-time library job, Moore responds: "The work I am doing and the annoyances to which I am subjected, are to some extent the goose that lays the golden egg and are I am sure, responsible just now, for any gain that I make toward writing. I have no swiftness . . . [but] I have I think, an intuition as to how I am to succeed if I do succeed." She can do without fame as well, although in the end she didn't have to: "I have no sympathy with people who find unpopularity embittering." And best of all she can respect her own virtues. She says in the famous "water-closet" letter to Elizabeth Bishop that she herself would not use the word in a poem because "I can't care about all things equally, I have a major effect to produce, and the heroisms of abstinence are as great as the heroisms of courage, and so are the rewards." Such strenuous amalgams of rigor and rhetoric abound in the letters, exalting restraint and insisting upon the highest and hardest road: "Patient or impatient repudiating of life, just repudiates itself. . . . What can be exciting to others is one's struggle with what is too hard," she exhorts the young (and apparently life-repudiating) Allen Ginsberg in 1952.

It is her inner clarity, one suspects, that allows Moore to put up with the lifelong charge that she writes obscurely, and indeed to stare down her own distaste for the great price directness must pay if she is to achieve the "implication" she requires. As far back as her Bryn Mawr days (Class of '09) she is accused of being "incoherent" and is discouraged from majoring in English.

She says to Warner (addressed as "Winks" in this playful 1941 letter—she'd be in her fifties by then): "I rekkonize my trouble as being too oblique & obscure, as a result of hating Crudeness (& . . . condescension and insulting didacticism). . . . And *I shall endeavor* to be CLEARER." But of course one can only be as clear, as she writes to her niece, as one's "natural reticence allows."

Her letters, which can seem the most mandarin, fussy constructions, can also at any moment go straight to the heart of the hardest subject. Her eerie assessment of Wallace Stevens in a letter to William Carlos Williams, for example, shows the privacies one oblique poet can sound in another: "Wallace Stevens is beyond fathoming, he is so strange; it is as if he had a morbid secret he would rather perish than disclose and just as he tells it out in his sleep, he changes into an uncontradictable judiciary with a gown and a gavel and you are embarrassed to have heard anything." Moore adores Stevens, mind you, confessing in a 1935 letter to Bryher that she has long secretly attempted "to bring my product into some sort of compatibility with Wallace Stevens." It is when she writes of Stevens more than in any other of her judgments that one feels she is appraising herself. "His great accuracy

and refracted images and averted manner indicate to
me a certain interior reconcentration of being. One
who has borne heat and burden as well as he has, and
as long as he has, is very deeplaid."

Moore sensed her own depths early, when still at
Bryn Mawr. The letters of the young are one of the
special thrills that volumes of letters offer, giving us the
sense of being there when the self and the self's powers are
still novelties worth remarking upon, before the poet has
grown accustomed to her nature. She writes to a friend,
"I have 'encysted' myself as far as the general world goes.
I fairly sparkle inside now and then, to think how real
is the world of fancy." Later, of course, she would never
mention such a thing. In Moore's college letters one
sees her just beginning to realize that her literary subject
matter isn't going to be the "red-hot stuff." Instead she
inclines to elusive subjects such as the jellyfish, which
she addresses in a manner already timelessly Mooreish:
"An amber-colored amethyst / Inhabits it."

Everything makes Marianne Moore's letters worth
reading. Thanks to her many reviews for the little maga-
zines of the twenties and especially to her editorship
of the *Dial* between 1925 and 1929, she knew slews of
modernist writers and knew them early. Later, when she

was an established poet and later still a *Life* magazine-size personality, she came to know second, third, and fourth waves of poets, enjoying correspondence of varying degrees of intimacy with Auden, famously with Elizabeth Bishop, also with James Merrill, and even with Allen Ginsberg. One admires the Byzantine courtesies Moore could elaborate to deflect the unwanted attentions of admirers or the fulminations of difficult friends such as Ezra Pound, a poet whom she staunchly admired but from whom she took no guff. She also counted as friends William Carlos Williams, T. S. Eliot, and the sometime couple H.D. and Bryher whom she and her mother took straight to their hearts. Mother and daughter enjoyed the literary people they knew in the old-fashioned way, eager for regular news of their families, however remote the domestic combinations might be from the Moores' own Presbyterian conservatism.

Of course one of the most toothsome pleasures of reading letters, and particularly the letters of a writer of such forbidding brilliance, is getting to peep behind the scenes. One relishes passages such as this in which she retails for Warner's amusement a moment of social distress: after her mother has urged her to go up and speak with W. B. Yeats following one of his New York lectures,

Moore realizes that "I had on my house-dress which has on the light blue trimming the ineradicable vestiges of a cod-liver oil spot." Our pleasure is compounded by MM's inability to phrase even the report of an oil spot on her dress in language natural to anyone else.

The Selected Letters astonish us with how deep the signature runs in Marianne Moore and humble us with how inexplicable it remains. Hers is a genius so perfectly self-tuned that we find ourselves laughing, one of the body's natural responses to shock.

I Demand
to Speak with God

Reading Frost's private notebooks is the opposite of pulling back the curtain on Oz. While the real Oz turns out to be a little man working a big speaker system, the real Frost turns out to be someone naturally—preternaturally—amplified even when nobody else is listening. *The Notebooks of Robert Frost* is his collected scraps, none of it written for an audience; it is the not-poetry, not-letters, not-lectures; it is the teacher's booklists and lecturer's notes, private reminders, scotched ideas, trial balloons, epigram practice sheets, scraps of plays and drafts of poems, fulminations and less-than-fulminations—all exactly as they came, except no longer in Frost's blocky hand (though his ink colors are duly noted). Over the course of 688 pages of them Frost has the answer for

The Notebooks of Robert Frost, edited by Robert Faggen (Belknap Press of Harvard University Press, 2006)

everything and the counter question—repeated to the Fth power. The voice that comes through even this fractured note-jotting is so supersaturated with authority that one winds up amazed that Frost was able to get down from his horse long enough to write the most beautiful American poems of the twentieth century.

If you're looking for Lionel Trilling's terrifying Frost of despair and desert places, you seldom find him here. This most private Frost turns out to be pretty much the Frost Frost promoted. In the notebooks we get the whole Yankee prop room—the idioms ("He opened his mouth a hundred dollars too soon on a lot of cows"), the good sense, the saltiness, the feisty independence, the belligerent pride in a new country that isn't all "run out" the way Europe is. (He'd like to "blow Shakespeare out of the language" for the way he's overawed our writers.) Really, the notebook Frost is surprisingly *un*dark, *un*lost—un*private*.

Yes, sorry to say there is precious little gossip-worthy private revelation despite the periodic turbulence of Frost's life. No familial discord, no word of his son's suicide, no late-life fascination with Kay Morrison, no machinations to get his gay colleague fired or other dastardly plots we'd like to know more about. And more surprising, when you think about Frost's poetry, is the utter absence of nature notes—no birches, no birds, no weather, no interest in rock wall construction. And something else that's missing is chronology. The entries really are a frustrating scramble. It turns out that Frost packed around with him over the years a satchel full of these undated notebooks (there are ultimately forty-eight, each here archivally described and transcribed) and continued not only to thumb through them but to add to them, so that entries next to each other in a "Brown soft paper cover spiral bound flip pad, 4⅛" × 6". Ruled pages" might have been written thirty years apart. You just don't know unless a pre-WWI reference happens to be followed by a New Deal reference. In his hyper-thorough and interesting notes (a pleasure in themselves), the editor, Robert Faggen, tips us off to such markers when he can.

There is a whole category of poets who are the "talking-back" poets, getting much of their energy from disagreeing or taking exception. Frost is at the top of the list. Frost always has to have this pushback he's writing against. He can argue harder; he can put all his force on one side; and he doesn't need to be fair. Plus it's fun. We know he's talking about himself when he advises, "Take an extreme position for the fun of battle." His natural rhetorical stance is dialogue, even when he's the only one talking, in which case he calls it "Self-repartee" or "my part in a conversation in which the other part is more or less implied." Frost never doubts the generative potential of his own mind: "The best mind asks and answers his own questions not the questions asked by others." Here's a typical bit of Frost fun:

> I demand to speak with God
>
> What is your business with God
>
> I couldn't explain that to anybody but God
>
> There is not God
>
> So much the better perhaps. Because that rules out half my business. If there is no God there can be no future life. The present life is all I should have to worry about.

However, if there does happen to be a live enemy on the other side, he also relishes that: "something fierce . . . rises in me at the sight of someone trying to get the better of me." Resistance is primary to everything about Frost: "Life catches on something to resist itself." Much of Frost's vitality comes from a desire to beat the other guy—and everybody's the other guy: "God too is out to win." He maintains in his *Paris Review* interview that for him, inspiration is "mostly animus."

The constant black hat can get to be a tiresome pose. It's as though the suspicious part of Frost saw every beautiful thing that he was capable of as a rock to throw. The reader must forever remember that whatever stance Frost takes, in the notebooks as elsewhere, virtuous or vile, you can be sure he'll sooner or later say it's a pose or a trick. Here, under the notebook heading "The Self-torturer," is an unsparing piece of what appears to be self-analysis (masked as "we") which undoes his entire claim to goodness and sense: "We have a reputation for good sense for kindness of heart. . . . Our good sense has been a gift for making phrase and . . . proverb (we have never known what we were doing). Our kindness of heart has been only dramatic and in general (Our follies have entailed great suffering)." And you see him repeatedly brand his humor "the most engaging cowardice. With it I myself have been able to hold some of my enemies in play far out of gunshot." There's something poisonous or at least reductive in his chronic insistence on this combative stance, and if we take it too seriously we're fooled into thinking Frost is smaller than he is.

Of course, in the beginning Frost had reasons to style himself a fighter, even if later it comes to feel like a bad habit. He wrote much of his greatest poetry (most of the first three books, he says) before he'd published any or had a lick of recognition. All he looked like was a bad chicken farmer. I was moved by what must have been an early note in which he says he's been "accused of talking as if to an audience when I have none."

He was lonely, but he also felt that he needed to be alone: "Don't go near anyone until you are strong-selfed enough not to be too much influenced," he says. We see his struggle to justify himself to himself and answer the imagined criticisms: "Why is it any more sincere and less hypocritical to . . . give up and sink back into what we came out of than to strain forward to what we are going to become?" It could be argued that Frost prevailed as a poet precisely because he could hold out alone. And who among us knows how to quit a behavior after it's done its job? Then too, maybe he never needed to be such a sharp operator in the first place; he considers this from the distance of the third person: "He [Frost] thought he was prevailing by . . . sheer worldly force and shrewdness, the traits that as a poet he wasn't supposed to have. . . . But all the time he was really a good poet and got . . . no inch further than his poetry made way for him." But the thing is, he liked being a sharp operator—mounting letter-writing campaigns to secure the good opinion of influential critics for his early books; undermining poets, including Edward Arlington Robinson and Carl Sandburg, whom he saw as serious rivals; and on one unequaled occasion going so far as to "accidentally" start a little fire on stage at Bread Loaf just as Archibald MacLeish was launching into his biggest crowd-pleaser.

In the notebooks Frost displays a kind of mind that thinks in PowerPoint, generating stays against confusion almost before there was any confusion. He repeats to himself what he insisted on publicly: "Nothing [is] more composing than composition," and in fact the phrase is the first line of Frost's final notebook. More tenderly he says, "To me any little form ~~is velvet~~." Generally, however, the form is more Sharpie than velvet. His notebook thinking runs to arrows, vectors, circles, bull's-eyes, ascending trajectories, descending trajectories. "There is a . . . life trajectory from less to more," he says in one place, and makes a little chart of the subcategories of this general truth: "From little or no family to more family," and the same with money,

fame, understanding, assurance, personality, and phy-
sique. Unremarkable aperçus like this become interesting
exactly because they are so unremarkable; Frost really
likes the sensation of drawing a grid over life. And it
makes sense; if you're going to be losing your way—
which is half of the definition of being a poet—isn't it
good to have some cardinal points to come back to?

And the points are very cardinal. Frost likes to
think about really big systems (democracy, socialism,
utopianism, Darwinism) and argue with the great points
of the great books. Philosophers are set up just well
enough to be slapped—or slapped on the back. You must
have systems to fight systems, and the bigger the system
you take on, the bigger fellow you are when you knock
it over. Actually, Frost sounds just like what he was—an
autodidact, essentially, with the pugnacity of the self-
taught-and-proud-of-it. He sees the independent mind
as constantly under attack: "You have to make your
mind up fresh every day just as you do your bed." The
fact that he was a college dropout (because "I was in a
trance with poetry that made it as distasteful to listen
to [teachers] talking about poetry as it would have been
to read Freud . . . when I was in love") combined with
his long career as the country's first poet in residence

on various college campuses (which he respells—more
correctly—as "Poet in resistance") predisposed him
to note (and note and note) how little wisdom is got
through specialization. He says in his *Paris Review* interview, "I'm not thorough. I hate the idea that you have
to read the whole of anybody." Frost is a big advocate
of pace. It's not so important to think things out in all
their detail as it is to keep going forward, jumping from
peak to peak without looking down.

A counterforce to Frost's zeal for abstractions is
his hair-trigger gift for concocting epigrams that make
his big ideas instantly physical. Thinking very broadly
about what makes America tick, as he loves to do (also
what makes Russia tick and France and England tick
as well as their major philosophers, writers, scientists,
forms of government, and historical ages), he says,
"This . . . country is a very broad pan to be only human
nature deep. . . . Try to move it and opinion rushes all
to one side and slops over." Or take this bit of wisdom
extracted from his teaching—not yet a polished epigram, but a striking image: a student "squeezed almost
too tight in school" is like an apple pip that goes farther
into the world "the tighter it has been pinched between
the fingers." An analogy machine where the turnover

time is next to nothing, Frost appears to have suffered
very little un-self-mediated experience.

Frost's propensity to think in terms of opposites
and pairs is so automatic that at its worst it feels for-
mulaic ("Civilization is the opposite of Utopia," and
the like). Of course I'm not the first to complain; Frost
says the same thing in his poem "To a Thinker," which
spoofs his habit of mind: "You call this thinking, but it's
walking. / Not even that, it's only rocking," the poem
accuses, and continues with a perfect menu of Frost's
own hobbyhorsical favorites:

> From force to matter and back to force,
> From form to content and back to form,
> From norm to crazy and back to norm,
> From bound to free and back to bound,
> From sound to sense and back to sound.

It isn't so much a poem as it is a lecture in couplets—with
the exception of its famous line and a half: "It almost
scares / a man the way things come in pairs." There
it is: a sudden Frost-drop down through the floor of
the poem and into the mind's weird pair-making propensity, with its mirrored hall of couplings, some of
which we'd rather not know about. And, by the way,

it is pleasant to observe how one deeply reverberating line-and-a-half can save a whole poem from oblivion. Frost felt a poem didn't have to be all great all the way through—momentum could make up for the bumps—but the ratio in "To a Thinker" is exceptionally encouraging for poets with bad spots.

The abstractions bounce back and forth from pole to pole with such regularity that sometimes I have to remind myself that the other Frost, the Frost who can say "No end so final [that it doesn't open] into further form," will soon be back. I suppose what we learn is that Frost is just like other people—only more so. His thinking is more intensely polar but the poles are less intensely stable. He calls poetry as well as life the "union of opposites," wherein compromise is doom: don't "get stuck in the golden mean." The most exciting or vital condition for Frost is some exquisite standoff where he's always feeling for—not attaining, mind you—a kind of balance, "missed and compensated; . . . missed almost saved and missed again." It's a sensation almost more muscular than mental; the poem is "the tremor of the deadlock." He wants to press thoughts, run them out to the point where they either self-destruct or turn around and become their opposites. And he loves the end of the

world, revisiting it frequently, imagining how socialism would crash it, or idealism. (It was clearly no great
strain for him to imagine two perishings in "Fire and
Ice.") Frost's a reasoner free to enjoy himself because
he knows reason will break down. We're "framed up"
to fail and he counts on that.

I have said that the notebooks don't generally trade
in darkness, but very occasionally there is a big, igneous
rip: "I am not sorry but rather enlarged that through
me life must stab someone," he says, apropos of nothing. And peppering the notebooks is the phrase "Dark
Darker Darkest" standing alone, as though it were a
code for something he kept working at in his mind.
(The editor offers some context for it, but this doesn't
explain away its perseverance.) On one occasion Frost
does begin developing what he means—venturing
well past the usual sparring tenor of the notebooks
and touching the dangerously marshy places usually
reserved for his best poems:

> Here where we are life wells up as a strong . . . spring
> perpetually . . . piling water on water . . . with the
> dancing high lights upon it. But it flows away on
> all sides as into a marsh of its own making. It flows

> away into poverty into insanity into crime. . . . Dark
> as it is there are these sorrows and darker still that
> we can do so little to get rid of them . . . the dark-
> est is that perhaps we ought not to want to get rid of
> them. . . . What life . . . craves most is signs of life.

In Frost's *poetry*, of course, this flowing away and draining off of original strength is a deep, repeated thought (and fear). Think of how everything golden "goes down" in "Nothing Gold Can Stay," or even better think of Frost's dazzling and diabolical poem "Spring Pools," where dark powers "blot out and drink up and sweep away" the freshets of life. Such a rare patch of deep probing in the notebooks, ending in a pronouncement ("What life craves most is signs of life"), lets us see the greater genius of his poems. In the notebooks, Frost moves quickly to the abstract; in the poem, he steers clear of the abstract altogether and instead overloads nature till dark stuff drips out the bottom. Frost is riveting, prose or poetry, but in the poetry the rivets rust through. A poem by its nature operates beyond rational control, which is a great service to a mind as controlling as Frost's. A poem means you're in too deep. In "Spring Pools," for all its balanced, reflected imagery of pools and flowers and all its tidy buttoned-up rhyming, Frost has got himself just where he craves to be—in an elemental battle where he's not the boss. The best form can do is serve as a barricade, giving the illusion of containment to the forces he's unleashed.

Predictably, where we find the biggest quantity of the subtlest thinking in the notebooks is in Frost's writing about poetry. Regarding poetry Frost speaks with profound and fascinating authority and cannot be tiresome. His double vision of metaphor alone—calling it the foundation of all understanding and at the same time counting on it to fail ("Every metaphor breaks down")—gives a nicely mystical crack to his poetical systems. He's always trying to catch the elusive cross-forces of sound and sense working within the poem, as here: "Sentences [in a poem] have a direction of their own back and forth across the penny under the paper. The idea comes out in lines almost at right angles to the lines of the sentences." Applied to poetry, you see the characteristic Frost-vectors ("back and forth," "at right angles") take on a strange metaphysical warp. Every equal sign has to get tilted funny.

In an intriguing example of how Frost's thinking circles around until one thing becomes another, in one notebook entry "meaning" loses its meaning and

becomes instead something that applies pressure to tone.
Writing about how a poem is made he says:

> The sound is everything. The best means of achiev-
> ing it are vowels consonants . . . verbal accent meter
> but the best of all for variety . . . is meaning. Great
> thoughts are of value as they supply profound tones.

In other words, in this bit of thinking, meaning has no
"meaning" value but rather imparts to a poem a kind
of useful basso quality. This is a savagely aesthetic point
of view and a surprising one when you think of Frost's
weakness for too *much* meaning in his lesser poems.
Which may be why he needed to dethrone it from
time to time. Certainly in other moods he esteemed the
point of a poem very highly—and esteemed his own
passion for point-making, arguing that it was necessary
to develop this habit in speech and prose or "how can
you expect them to occur to you in the emergency
of . . . poems." And of course whether at any particular
moment Frost is pro-sense or pro-sound is of much less
interest to him than that he isn't in the gormless middle.

The question I kept considering in reading this
giant mess of scraps was: What am I finding out that I

couldn't learn elsewhere? Little I've mentioned so far does more than confirm what we already knew; it's all in his poems, introductions, and lectures—and there it's in complete sentences. Of course in reading the notebooks some things are underscored. For example, so many of his notes are in dialogue that your appreciation deepens for how elemental dialogue really is to Frost's mind. And the many lists of course and lecture ideas underscore what a big part of his life teaching and lecturing were. And naturally you see lots of rewriting and can watch Frost giving his work its signature physical and idiomatic punch, even in such a small sample as this: "~~when they were absent~~ behind their backs." But the main thing one discovers in the notebooks is Frost's great fidelity to himself. Over the long project of reading this lifetime of notes (nearly a lifetime itself) you see how long a poet can stay fascinated by an image or thought, how he gets hooked and can't get unhooked—whether he ever can make anything from the image or not; how he works his ideas over decades, how he favors them, how he develops a limp for them.

Wang-Pang-Woo-
Poo-Woof-Woof

I got my opinion of poet Wallace Stevens nailed down at just about the same time that the *Letters* first came out. As an undergraduate, and having analyzed the obligatory clutch of Stevens's poems to a contextual nub, I was convinced that there was a single master combination that I had figured out which would throw all of the poet's empty but imposing safes open to me.

Well, age and nine hundred pages of letters have softened my stand. While it remains true that Stevens is endlessly fingering the tumblers of the big imagination-versus-reality lock, and that some things do get to looking terribly familiar, I no longer believe that I'm so smart and he's so not. My adolescent impatience with all things antinomic has converted to sturdy admiration

---

Letters of Wallace Stevens, edited by Holly Stevens (University of California Press, 1981)

and—perhaps more—affection, both for the man and for his immense and stubborn endeavor. Even saying "stubborn" makes me feel I have wronged a friend. For I now freely acknowledge that Stevens never had a choice. He was never released from the center of the struggle between the claims of the mind and the claims of the world.

Wallace Stevens is in the same fix his whole life. His earliest dandified letters to his mother are true to a natural-born thinker who cannot bear much more than the flowers and zithers of the physical world. He is collecting and practicing language—as he must—for the private speech his nature requires. But as we see from his early journal entries, he understands also that he is a conventional sort of person who must fit in socially, a person who will require the pleasant things that take money. Although his pleasures come only from what is "unsullied," he must compromise, he tells himself, perhaps becoming a "bustling merchant" or a "money-making lawyer." "We must, come down, we must use tooth and nail," he chants to himself. Young Stevens is a wonderful paradox. He accuses himself of cold "artificiality" and aesthetic distaste for the world, and yet he is also physically vigorous, "a hearty Puritan" who grows to six foot two and can hike a whopping forty-two miles in a day. But of course when he gets to his destination he may not like it; by the age of twenty-three he is already saying, "The sea is loveliest far in the abstract when the imagination can feed upon the idea of it. The thing itself is dirty, wobbly and wet."

After his student days at Harvard and brief sallies into journalism and independent law practice, Stevens settles in lifelong as an executive with the Hartford Accident and Indemnity Company. He marries Elsie—a lovely and unlettered creature who had quit high school to play piano in the sheet music section of a department store, with whom he has carried on a five-year epistolary courtship—and sets them up in a fine house within walking distance of the office. Eventually there is a daughter, Holly, who will become the editor of the *Letters*. It is exactly the mild and regulated life he requires.

It seems altogether fitting that Stevens's life should divide early into two hermetic parts, one half the businessman and one half the poet. Stevens was a genius of accommodation: rather than being torn to shreds by his antithetical parts, he just doubled himself. He figured out a way to achieve a very enduring, serviceable equilibrium, living his requirement for office routine, domestic quiet, and financial security, and jobbing out the impulses that wouldn't fit.

As a creature of endless desire, he puts himself on a slow desire-drip. He is always trying to control his appetite for a life of motion and travel, persuading himself that "perhaps, it is best . . . that one should have only glimpses of reality," and as much as he can discouraging himself from wanting: "For all I know, thinking of a roasted duck, or a Chinese jar or a Flemish painting may be quite equal to having one." Throughout his life he exchanges letters with travel surrogates in Cuba, France, Ireland, and elsewhere, desiring the world of them, as in this letter to a favorite young Cuban: "What I really like to have from you is not your tears on the death of Bernanos, say, but news about chickens raised on red peppers." He has endless packages—carved figurines in a "box from Peking" or tea from "Wang-Pang-Woo-Poo-Woof-Woof"—shipped to him by a network of friends of friends living abroad. The letters acknowledging these casks and cartons are among his most delighted. In his own domestic travels for Hartford insurance, Stevens's favorite destination is the Florida Keys, where he for once finds an exoticism equal to his imagination. On one illustrative occasion he enjoys a light repast of "doves on toast," which would have made a good title for one of his poems. One feels the insatiability of his appetites for unfamiliar things. In the quiet rooms of his pleasant Hartford home he breathes up their foreign air, so essential to his established domestic bliss.

Stevens must order out for fresh air from the world of reality, but in the world of poetry he generates his own. And for a long time he doesn't seem to need to write any letters about it. It is startling then to encounter his first letter to Harriet Monroe, editor of *Poetry*, who is the first to accept his work. It is 1914 and he is thirty-five. He tells her, "My autobiography is, necessarily, very brief; for I have published nothing." How has he become a poet without us knowing? We have had little hint beyond a half-embarrassed admission to his wife in 1913 that he has been "trying to get together a little collection of verses." Yet somehow he has secretly evolved from the writer of negligible packets of love poems for his wife-to-be into the Wallace Stevens we know.

Stevens explains his "obscurity" as an interim con-dition: "I wish rather desperately to keep on dabbling and to be as obscure as possible until I have perfected an authentic and fluent speech for myself." His letters repeat again and again this ferocious desire not to be untrue to himself. He does not mean to be cautious as he is in real life. Referring to the poem of which he pronounced himself fondest, "The Emperor of Ice-Cream," he says, "I dislike niggling, and like letting myself go. This [poem] represented what was in my mind at the moment, with the least possible manipulation." By his own report, he writes easily. He is so focused and imaginatively hair-triggered that he hardly remembers what he's written later and dislikes looking back. He does feel, however, that his inclination to abstraction is a danger for him and likens his case to "the boy whose mother told him to stop sneezing; he replied: 'I'm not sneezing; it's sneezing me.'"

Stevens's predispositions make a weird combination, fostering a poetry that is at the same time abstract and sensorially immediate, with none of the great, warm middle range of the personal. Still, even if one prefers the personal (as I do not) it is hard to stay impatient. In the *Letters* one feels the immensity of his ambition for poetry—to provide a spiritual compass in a drifting world: "Certainly, if civilization is to consist only of man himself, and it is, the arts must take the place of divinity." Stevens argues that "a competent poem introduces order," and that order brings "peace." Although this peace is an illusion, it brings a necessary "freshen-ing of life." He is impatient with poets who "have no conception of the importance of the thing. . . . The world never moves at a very high level, but a few men should always move at a very high level."

Stevens's poems have a hilarity that isn't funny, a *joie* without the *vivre*. In the *Letters* it is great fun to hear him trying to explain his exuberant private yelps. Illu-minating "The Man with the Blue Guitar" for an Italian professor, he patiently reveals that "this-a-way and that-a-way and ai-yi-yi are colloquialisms. . . . A man who is master of the world balances it on his nose this way and that way and the spectators cry ai-yi-yi." Such yelps were native to Stevens's speech since he wrote letters as a boy to his mother (he transcribes the "tink-a-tink-a-tink-tink-a-a-a" of his brother's mandolin playing) and as a young suitor, serenading Elsie with the inflaming rhythms of "Rig-a-jig-jig / And a jig-jig-jig." They have always been rather lonely sounds. But loneliness is not the grief for poets that it is for others. Says Stevens, "Poets are never lonely even when they pretend to be."

In reading the *Letters* we warm to Stevens in a way his poems alone are less likely to warm us, not so much because we are able to see him sitting in Elsie's flower garden, or bringing a cake to his grandson, or remorseful at having said something perhaps too personal to Marianne Moore after one too many cocktails, but because we truly see that the difficult Wallace Stevens we sense from the poems was not a pose or a reduction but a brave and unrelenting articulation of his own impossibility. Late in the letters he describes to a friend the robins and doves that sit on his chimney before sunrise; he says they are "connoisseurs of daylight before the actual presence of the sun coarsens it." I, for one, have no trouble making out a bulky old insurance man perched right up there with them in the pearly dawn.

The Trail of the
Hunted Wolf

Nobel Prize–winning poet Joseph Brodsky was born to be posthumous. He groomed himself for it, spending his life vigorously dismissing the facts of life, discounting "what happened," shaking off biography. He bent his prodigious talents to keeping his life provisional and to resisting "collection"—professing himself eager to have his poetry misarranged by future editors, after the fashion of the fragments of the classical Greeks and Romans: "The fate of an ancient author, Archiloches or someone. All that's left of him is rats' tails. There's a fate I could envy." Brodsky's poetry is riddling, elusive, shape-shifting, and compulsively playful. Hounded first by the KGB and later by his own fame, he was a man playing catch-me-if-you-can, a man whose only safety

Conversations with Joseph Brodsky: A Poet's Journey Through the Twentieth Century, by Solomon Volkov, translated by Marian Schwartz (The Free Press, 1998)

lay in never going to ground, a man for whom the best solution was dissolution. Brodsky invited being broken up precisely because he knew that language—which is what mattered supremely to him, and, he insisted, should to all of human ambition—will always find and reassemble itself. His great dazzling puzzle will go together many ways and all of them right.

One could almost hope that Brodsky's conversations with Solomon Volkov would prove less blinding than his two collections of essays, *Less Than One* and *On Grief and Reason*, which should be read through a welder's mask. But alas, while Volkov and Brodsky do spend a certain amount of time catching up on their common Leningrad memories—of blessedly mild interest to American readers—the sparks otherwise fly. In 1978, Volkov, a musician steeped in Russian literature and a fellow émigré, got the idea of recording these conversations with Brodsky in their native tongue (now gracefully translated). Neither poet nor academic, Volkov was not another remora looking for a ride, and this he believes made him attractive to Brodsky. The project extended over fifteen years. Volkov turned out to be the perfect sparring partner for Brodsky, exercising him hard enough to make him sweat.

It couldn't have been an easy relationship. In his excellent introduction, Volkov describes the Brodsky of those early years, the "lone wolf of Russian litera-ture . . . a hunted wolf, aggressively baring his fangs to drive back the pressing chase." He reports that even casual meetings with Brodsky "had an upsetting effect" on people: "There were always overtones of menace." At one point Volkov and an émigré friend confess to one another that they have each gotten nosebleeds after "long tête-à-têtes with Brodsky."

Volkov assembles twelve conversations which loosely follow the history of the poet's life and gener-ally radiate out from Brodsky's passion for one writer or another. Although pieced together from zillions of hours of tape, the conversations come across as seamlessly elastic and alive. It's hard to imagine how Brodsky could have placed himself more securely at the cultural heart of Rus-sian/Western history in the second half of this century. The titles Volkov gives to the dozen conversations tell the tale: A Leningrad Youth; Marina Tsvetaeva; Arrests, Asylums, and a Trial; Exile to the North; Robert Frost; Persecution and Expulsion; W. H. Auden; Life in New York and the Defection of Alexander Godunov; Italy and Other Travels; Remembering Anna Akhmatova;

Rereading Akhmatova's Letters; and St. Petersburg: Memories of the Future.

It is particularly ironic that one who disdains the importance of external reality ("I think the individual should ignore circumstances")—one who believes that thoughts are secreted from within rather than coming from outside the self—should have so much history tied like tin cans to his tail. He can never outrun it. As the legendary Akhmatova herself observed after Brodsky was sentenced in a sensationally absurd Soviet trial to five years of internal exile in the frozen North, "What a biography they're creating for our redhead! You'd think he'd hired them." But however extraordinary the events of Brodsky's life, his reactions are consistently more extraordinary. It is not that he is unflappable—he flaps a lot, but never when you expect. Is he horrified by being thrown into a cell by the KGB? Not at all. "I actually liked it pretty well. It's true, I liked it! Because it was a one-man cell." Is he crazed when on his first night in an insane asylum the man in the next cot "slit his veins"? Not nearly as crazed as he is by the aesthetically maddening way in which space was organized in the room: "To this day I don't know what was wrong. Either the windows were slightly smaller than usual, or else the ceilings were too low. Or else the beds were too big. . . . This violation of proportions drove me crazy." Is he scarred by the famous trial that catapulted him to international fame as a poet martyr? "Believe me, it made absolutely no impression on me whatsoever. Really, none whatsoever!" If Brodsky skitters away from any admission of vulnerability and often seems to be posturing, it's easy to see why. He knows that to dwell on or dramatize his oppression by the great faceless Soviet is to enter into the same kind of thinking the state uses. Brodsky just won't play right; the state's rules are nonsense to him. And if he won't be the victim, it can't be the master.

Brodsky's conversations with Volkov are bullet trains from the ridiculous to the sublime. In one single (perhaps condensed) monologue, Brodsky moves from the bizarre idea that "a significant percentage of the support for Stalin among intelligentsia in the West had to do with their latent homosexuality" (they were attracted to his sexy mustache) to a heady analysis of Mandelstam's satiric "Ode," a poem famous for tweaking the untweakable Stalin. Brodsky describes how Mandelstam carries off "the same trick" against Stalin that the Russian fortune-teller does against her customer when she "dives into your face"; Mandelstam "violated [Stalin's] distance, he violated that same territorial imperative. . . . To say nothing of the poem's phenomenal aesthetics: cubist, almost posterlike." A feral scent mixes with the smell of ether in all of Brodsky's musings: "if I were Stalin, I would have slit Mandelstam's throat immediately," concludes the Lone Wolf with animal relish.

In keeping with the light boxer's stance that Brodsky maintained against the world for his whole too-brief life (he died of a heart attack in 1996 at the age of fifty-five), the conversations dance with brilliant feints and shifts. But to me what soars above all else is the unshifting voice of Brodsky the seer, who simply knows secrets so pure and terrible that one feels that the ancient mask of poetry itself is speaking. In every way possible, grabbing his metaphors from the gutters and the galaxies, Brodsky insists upon language as the grail itself, and upon poetry as the great mental "accelerator," the door to whatever moral wisdom there might be. Language, for Brodsky, precedes and contains all; language is the god that commands *time* and *space*. The poet is used by language for the purposes of language; forget the poet's *life*. The only proof that he's right is how our clothes are burned off when we try to stand directly in front of his mind. It's not perfect proof, but it's persuasive.

Only Doubts

You could think of these lectures on poetry as either the Essential Borges or the Redundant Borges. Using a favorite Borgesian device by which infinity may be unfolded from a scrap of paper, perhaps all of Borges's work might be reconstituted from this little book in which he revisits many of his favorite ideas. ("A mere handful of arguments have haunted me all these years. I am decidedly monotonous," he has said elsewhere with characteristic self-effacement.) On the other hand, given the likely survival of Borges's books, it could be argued that these lectures are little more than a milky mirror reflection of mightier iterations, a handful of loosely organized talks filled with charming apologies for a blind man's "slips." They have the tone of Borges speaking more or less off the cuff to an obviously adoring Harvard audience for the 1967–68 Charles Eliot

This Craft of Verse, by Jorge Luis Borges, edited by Călin-Andrei Mihăilescu (Harvard University Press, 2000)

Norton Lectures. Their very tardy publication by Harvard University Press in 2000 ("transcribed from tapes only recently discovered," says the book jacket) encourages this suspicion that the lectures are a minor footnote to a profound body of work.

I was thinking this way when I started to read them. But then something crept up on me, and it was different from the sort of searing intellectual pleasure I recall from my first reading of Borges's fictions; it was instead a lovely lightness of spirit. Behind all the lectures I could feel Borges's abiding dream of deliquescing into the glories of literature. At first this was hard to see because it's mixed up with his worries about getting things a bit scrambled up, but then there it is, this big egolessness: Borges simply apprehends the inexhaustible radiance of literature and would walk into it naked and without a name, such a lover is he.

And that's another thing: there is an emphasis upon passion in these lectures and a reliance on feelings that is, I suppose I shouldn't say contrary to, but outside the universe of Borges's cool, impersonal, intellectually thrilling fictions. After all, Borges is a thinker who can squander what would be a dozen other writers' whole intellectual careers in a single story such as

"Tlön, Uqbar, Orbis Tertius." But here in these lectures
Borges's emphasis is never on the riddling intellect or
the understanding or the importance of meaning—all
of which he lets us know he mistrusts. He says, "When
I am writing something, I try not to understand it. I do
not think intelligence has much to do with the work of
a writer." He insists instead upon the physical apprehension of poetry, recalling the first impact of poetry upon
him as a boy (the poem was Keats's "On First Looking
into Chapman's Homer"), realizing that "it was not
happening to my mere intelligence but to my whole
being, to my flesh and blood." Borges is much quicker
to describe his experience of literature as a reader rather
than as a writer. "I think of myself as being essentially
a reader," he says. "I have ventured into writing, but I
think that what I have read is far more important than
what I have written. For one reads what one likes—yet
one writes not what one would like to write but what
one is able to write."

Borges is a nearly cuddly anti-pedant who won't
be grand or offer himself as an authority in spite of his
legendary erudition. In the first of the six lectures, "The
Riddle of Poetry," he immediately says he has no answers
to the riddle of poetry. In the final lecture, "A Poet's

Creed," he dispatches creeds, saying, "I have only a fal-
tering kind of creed. . . . In fact, I think of all poetic
theories as being mere tools for the writing of a poem."
He just as quickly dismisses the cherished illusion that a
master masters his craft: "Every time I am faced with a
blank page . . . I feel that I have to rediscover literature for
myself. But the past is of no avail whatever to me. . . . I
am nearing seventy. I have given the major part of my
life to literature, and I can offer you only doubts."

But for all his protestations, again and again I watch
Borges lightly tip in a thought—attaching it to the page
so casually that it might fall off—and feel it acquire
the loveliest sticking power. For example, at one point
Borges is pondering some favorite lines by Robert Frost,
noticing how Frost simply repeats the line "And miles
to go before I sleep" and pointing out how this leaves
the reader with the feeling that the second sleep is death.
He remarks upon how much more powerful this is than
clearly spelling out the point about death. Then he says,
just sort of by-the-by, as though this were not Borges's
own rhetorical method in these lectures, or were not
the very reason that all art refreshes us: "Because, as I
understand it, anything suggested is far more effective
than anything laid down. Perhaps the human mind has

a tendency to deny a statement." (Note his disarming "as I understand it.") And on goes the sweet meandering river of thought and association as Borges continues musing upon the virtue of suggestion:

> When something is merely . . . hinted at, there is a kind of hospitality in our imagination. We are ready to accept it. I remember reading, some thirty years ago, the works of Martin Buber—I thought of them as being wonderful poems. Then . . . I found, . . . much to my astonishment, that Martin Buber was a philosopher and that all his philosophy lay in the books I had read as poetry. Perhaps I had accepted those books because they came to me through poetry, through suggestion, through the music of poetry, and not as arguments.

Something that fascinates me is the constant feeling of blurring, or interpenetration, of categories throughout the lectures. One feels in Borges a kind of advanced mental permeability that's gotten way beyond smart. It shows up in so many ways. In the Martin Buber story above, for example, Borges savors the mix-up of poetry and philosophy, delighting precisely in the vibrating borders where categories lose their meaning. The truth of beauty is always the central concern for Borges, and it is almost a plasma, everywhere and nowhere at once, and decidedly nobody's property. Nor is poetry fixed. "Poetry is a new experience every time. Every time I read a poem, the experience happens to occur. And that is poetry." I love that phrase, "happens to occur," with its feeling of chance and magic and pure lack of inevitability. There is always this feeling in Borges that whatever is up is fresh—a new sensation or idea. Borges is always just now thinking something: "I am thinking," he says, or "I thought this three or four days ago." Every thought arises precariously and mysteriously out of nothing—though, of course, it is a nothing lavishly appointed with an array of classical, early, and modern languages and a remarkable quantity of memorized poetry.

Borges also happily blurs the distinction between literature in its original language and in translation, pointing out that poetry, rather than being what is *lost* in translation, is sometimes *gained*: "It might be said that no original is needed. Perhaps a time will come when a translation will be considered as something in itself." For the sanguine Borges the ancient tree of literature is both the sacred blossomer and the source of cuttings that are just as good.

The poet, insists Borges, doesn't own the beauty of his works; it passes into him from "the Holy Ghost, from the subliminal self, or perhaps from some other writer. I often find I am merely quoting something I read some time ago and then that becomes a rediscovering. Perhaps it is better that a poet should be nameless." He is fascinated with the idea of literature as an endless series of variations on a few basic metaphors and stories, seeing the deep structure of literature itself as a sort of code, as though there were a common genetic marker that links all writers throughout time. It is the correspondences among works of literature that compels Borges, rather than the personal, biographical differences between their authors. The idea of unwitting replication—writers eternally reworking the same material—is of course familiar from Borges's unsettling fictions, but in these late lectures it feels so human. And reassuring.

In spite of Borges's many volumes of poetry and the fact that he considered himself a poet first, before a fabulist or essayist, I have nonetheless tended to think of him as a poet *last*. So it is lovely to be reminded of the fineness of his ear (educated early in English) and the delicacy of his discernment, as when, in supporting

his idea that translations can surpass originals, he enter-
tains the Latin tag *"Ars longa, vita brevis."* "Here," says
Borges dismissively, "we have a plain statement. . . . It
strikes no deep chord. In fact it is a kind of prophecy
of the telegram and of the literature evolved by it. 'Art
is long, life is short.'" Much later when Chaucer has
rewritten it as "The lyf so short, the craft so long to
lerne," Borges admires how

> we get not only the statement but also the very
> music of wistfulness. We can see that the poet is not
> merely thinking of the arduous art and of the brev-
> ity of life; he is also feeling it. This is given by the
> apparently invisible, inaudible key word—the word
> 'so.' 'The lyf *so* short, the craft *so* long to lerne.'

Again here is Borges, never content with the idea alone,
always looking after the music and feeling.

This Craft of Verse joins the timeless body of Borgesian thought whose circumference is everywhere and
whose center is whichever Borges you're reading at
the time. In this particular center, Borges is keen to
remind us that one cannot predict or establish how or
where the beautiful will manifest itself. And it is in the
end beauty that matters. "You may not agree with the

examples I have chosen," says Borges. "Perhaps tomorrow I may think of better examples, may think I might
have quoted better lines. But as you can pick and choose
your own examples, it is not needful that you care
greatly about Homer, or about the Anglo-Saxon poets,
or about Rossetti. Because everyone knows where to
find poetry. And when it comes, one feels the touch
of poetry, that particular tingling of poetry." Borges's
aesthetic "tingling" recalls Nabokov's famous "fris-
son." The sensation along the spine was probably much
the same for these similarly exhilarating masters who
grew old so differently—Nabokov becoming ever more
defended and riddling, Borges becoming ever more
transparent and universal.

Flying

I see Annie Dillard writing with a pen that has a dangerously generous flow; if she pauses for an instant, the ink begins spreading into the paper, branching like fine roots out into the white fibers. There is no moment not in peril of becoming permanent: "If I wish, and I do not, I can have never-to-be-repeated moments, however dreadful, anywhere and anytime," she says in her 1982 volume of essays, *Teaching a Stone to Talk.*

Clearly, material is no problem for Annie Dillard; she is assaulted by it, cracked open at a tap, catapulted easily into the spheres, plunged through ring on ring of consciousness. But if material is not a problem, direction might be. How does one move on—and why bother—when all terror and beauty are manifest at every point? And how achieve a bearable voice? Well, the history of her first sixteen years provides natural direction in *An*

An American Childhood, by Annie Dillard (Harper & Row, 1987)

American Childhood. And as to voice, that remains elastic, great-natured, and wild. Reading certain passages brings wind tears—the water forced off the surface of the eyes and straight back against the temples. You're up there, in that open cockpit, earth the sweetest arc below. Then you stall out, or maybe there's a vaudeville turn featuring a couple of rubes.

This is, at every bump and turn, an American childhood, and Norman Rockwell could not more lovingly render the articles of the native child's constitution. Take the hardball: "It took a grass stain nicely, stayed round, smelled good and lived lashed in your mitt all winter, hibernating." But, more specifically, it is an upper-class Pittsburgh childhood. Annie Dillard is the bright, healthy first child of rich, young, amusing parents. She is loved, instructed in the arts of humor and politesse, and prepared for the full glory of country-club dinner dances by way of the country-club swimming pool, the correct Presbyterian church, and the correct dancing classes where "we were foreordained to assemble, Friday after Friday, for many years until the distant and seemingly unrelated country clubs took over the great work of providing music for us later and later into the night until the time came when we should all have married each other up, at last."

Annie Dillard enjoys every advantage God and Pittsburgh could offer a child in the fifties. She suffers no external grief greater than exclusion from the all-boy baseball team, no horror greater than having to get up close to some nuns, with "those white boards like pillories with circles cut out and some bunched human flesh pressed like raw pie crust into the holes." It is a wonderfully fortunate childhood that paid off the way we'd hope they all would. She grows strong through private tests of a rigor only a child can impose. She stokes her passion for headlong effort, singleminded concentration, and blind rapture with the disciplines of pitching, drawing, rock and bug collecting, and detecting. Everything she picks up turns out to be "the hanging end of a very long rope." She recognizes the words of the novelists, naturalists, poets, philosophers, and God as the revolutionary documents they are.

Until she is shanghaied by adolescence, she is a more-than-biddable child. With good reason: her parents are even more agreeable than the coeval Cleavers. Of her pretty, prankish mother, Annie Dillard says, "Mother's energy and intelligence suited her for a greater role in a larger arena—mayor of New York, say." Her father is the tall, dreamy scion of American Standard who at one point converts his stocks to a powerboat to solo down the Allegheny River all the way to New Orleans. The two are well matched: restless, bright, essentially conventional, with a passion for American ingenuity and a moral commitment to the well-told joke. The three daughters are delighted audience and carefully instructed understudies.

Annie Dillard throws down the white glove at about the same time that she takes up boys. Her conscience, or perhaps her nouveau intellect, compels her to quit the Presbyterian church. And not by quiet boycott; this is a written proclamation, to her parents' horror. She, apparently alone, sees the untenable hypocrisy of the opulent church and the barefoot Christ: "After all, I was the intelligentsia around these parts, singlehandedly. The intelligentsium."

That's just the start. There's a whole lot of resisting that has to be done:

> In summer we girls commonly greeted each other, after a perfunctory hello, by extending our forearms side by side to compare tans. We were blond, we were tan, our teeth were white and straightened, our legs were brown and depilated, our blue eyes glittered pale in our dark faces. . . . It was not for

me. I hated it so passionately I thought my shoul-
ders and arms, swinging at the world, would split
off from my body like loose spinning blades, and fly
wild and slice everyone up.

Enter Rimbaud, drag races, and Annie Dillard's moment
in juvenile court. But however mean she feels, Annie
Dillard's history is never mean. She is amused, tender,
tolerant, and, of course, repeatedly knocked out by
what a rush life is.

We always hope the autobiographies of writers
will show where their characteristic *idées* were first
fixed. Annie Dillard does not disappoint. She relives
a series of first scenes which isolate themes to which
she will return through all her writing. We witness
the first triumph of observation over terror when the
five-year-old connects the bodiless monster caroming
night after night off her bedroom walls to the ordinary
car sounds outside; it was only the streetlight glancing
off a windshield. "Figuring it out was a long and forced
ascent to the very rim of being, to the membrane of
skin that both separates and connects the inner life and
the outer world." The terrifying "narrative fiction"
of the imagination is thus simplified, chastened, made

innocent of intention through willed attention to the world beyond the window. This is a major discovery for the child and one she has to keep making.

Annie Dillard occupies the primeval jungle of childhood, lit only intermittently by reason or by beauty. We see how her sense of beauty is first linked to courage, solitude, and mystery when she describes another event from the same period. She watches from inside the warm family dining room a "transfigured Jo Ann Sheehy, skating alone under the streetlight. . . . Under her skates the street's packed snow shone; it illumined her from below, the cold light striking under her chin." Here is a child, of poor Irish lineage by day, transformed in the killing cold night to a perfect vision of beauty. "Was everything beautiful so bold?" she asks. And always the answer is yes. There is always a daring to beauty, a perfection of act lifted whole from ordinary knowledge, installed forever in the archetypes.

We see also the first emblems of the spectacular energy Annie Dillard must always strive to control when the child watches electricity gush like water from a severed power cable and burrow with wasted force down into bubbling asphalt. And we see the first intimations of the writer's secret wealth awaiting the one child only. She finds a coin in the back-alley dirt. She knows this is only the top coin: there are more coins down there, growing more rare, mysterious, and precious layer to layer. And only she knows where to dig. "I decided to devote my life to unearthing treasure."

These are some of the patterns all the fabric of her days will be cut to. She says of her treasure-seeking schemes, "It was the long years of these same few thoughts that wore tracks in my interior life." But are there ever first things, first times? One senses even in her earliest memories other deeper strata of coins. One senses always that the thing that marks can, in some sense, only remark; that there was an Annie Dillard spirit compact on high, which came down and entered—perhaps to its surprise— a nice blond child. Perhaps one does not become oneself at all. Surely if one does, Annie Dillard will be the last to know, whose apprehension of beauty does not shift, whose vision—which spirals out to the fringes of the universe at the drop of a hat—cannot expand.

She is pierced by the identical mystery in all her writing. This is all very well for saints, but Annie Dillard was trained at her joke-loving parents' knees to respect a good story, watch the pacing, and hold a punch-line sacred. She is not a simple ecstatic who can let her eyes roll back in her head; she's got to give value for money, keep the show on the road. So what is a stand-up ecstatic to do? She puts on a variety show, with lots of scene shifts and sometimes a false mustache. Her voice shifts from the stuttering of angels to the merely enraptured; from the notes of the nascent naturalist to the captions of a 1952 *Life* photo-essay; from the homespun to the cold-blooded observations of the young child.

Have I said Annie Dillard is hilarious? She is. Here is the terrible child experimenting upon the innocent parental flesh: "Loose under their shinbones, as in a hammock, hung the relaxed flesh of their calves. You could push and swing this like a baby in a sling. Their heels were dry and hard, sharp at the curved edge. The bottoms of their toes had flattened. . . . I would not let this happen to me. Under certain conditions the long bones of their feet showed under their skin. The bones rose up long and miserably thin in skeletal rays on the slopes of their feet. This terrible sight they ignored also."

Annie Dillard uses her hypervision on everything. She has to; it's death to hide. This is a force we're dealing with here, a live cable whipping around. The ground is hot, and she's barefoot, and it means a lot of dancing. She can usually only manage to set us down in one spot for a few pages; then it's off to the next branding. Like all great writers, she is fresh, jarring, passionately dedicated to her subjects and attached to them only by a gossamer. It is earnest, the one and only, the real thing; it is a joke, it is arbitrary, it might as easily have been something else.

Or somewhere else. The setting of her childhood is thoroughly American—the totemic baseball mitt, the Pittsburgh steel mills, the confluence of great rivers with their freight of child-inflaming French and Indian history, the country club, the public library in the poor black section of the city, the free Carnegie art classes at the museum. But there is that ecstatic Annie Dillard ring off everything. She could get high C out of a potato. It is this ecstasy, or, more accurately, the management of this ecstasy, which seems the native ground of the book. "'Calm yourself,' people had been saying to me all my life." She is not calm. She is always asking—the question is born large in her—what does it feel like to be alive? "Living, you stand under a waterfall. . . . Can you breathe here . . . where the force is greatest . . . ? . . . Yes, you can breathe even here. You could learn to live like this." Let me revise; there *is* an attainable calm for Annie Dillard: in absolute attention. In the first essay in *Teaching a Stone to Talk* she locks eyes with a weasel; her mind mixes with his wild mind, and she knows his way for a moment: "open to time and death painlessly, noticing everything, remembering nothing, choosing the given with a fierce and pointed will."

There is always a feral scent to Annie Dillard's writing, and always a little spatter of blood—from birth, the kill, the dissection, the thorn of the rose. There are jaws, literal, figurative, and more figurative, gripping on past death. The terrible and the beautiful are studied with the same unblinking eye. In her Pulitzer Prize–winning *Pilgrim at Tinker Creek*, we see a frog sucked hollow from underneath by a giant water bug. In *An American Childhood*, the young Annie Dillard watches a great moth hatch in a Mason jar. The jar is too small for it to spread and dry its giant wings, and they are welded half-furled. Her teacher releases it with a flourish. She watches it hobble down the school drive. This image never stops haunting her.

But what image does? In another essay in *Teaching a Stone to Talk* she eats a dish containing the same sort of delicate deer which at that moment is struggling against a rope in the clearing before her. She eats with appetite and with the knowledge of suffering. She does not turn away from it or claim to understand it or deny that the meat is good. "It is a fact that the high level of lactic acid, which builds up in muscle tissues during exertion, tenderizes." She keeps it all before us, as she keeps the photograph of the twice-burned man's face before herself, tucked in her dresser mirror. "These things are not issues; they are mysteries."

Childhood is natural material for such a fierce spirit, whose words do not hope to correct, but to clarify—to praise as light does. And the headlong quality of her prose was surely bred in the bone. This girl meant to fly. In a wonderful passage in the autobiography, we see her flapping full gallop down Penn Avenue—to use up the joy inside her, to strain the ligatures of faith, to test the draw of courage, to fly through the face of dignity. It is quite a success. It has carried her all the way to now. And is she really flying? It feels like it.

The Abrasion of Loneliness

Marilynne Robinson's *Lila* describes the abrasion of loneliness, the scrubbing a person can take to all the surfaces of desire; it is the history of the hypersensitivities and bluntings that result from an almost but not quite absolute absence of nurturing. It demonstrates, as only such extremity can, the quick availability of kinds of salvation: it takes just a smidgeon of love to land on the starveling's tongue and the starveling is fed-enough, one more time. The smallest gestures, the most ordinary objects, are triggers to these salvations. The wine and wafer are all over the place.

Lila is about outsides and insides and how poorly they're matched up most of the time and how much we want that fixed. But at the same time Lila is just as much witness to the strange privileges of the outsider: the tolerance—which actually becomes an appetite—for

Lila, by Marilynne Robinson (Farrar, Straus & Giroux, 2014)

wandering; the radiance holding its breath in any old thing; the looseness of the self, or the loosening of the self, I might say, that fits with the looseness out there. It approaches an apprehension of namelessness—which is terrible and a relief.

So maybe we don't want outside and inside matched up, or we don't trust that they could be without something too important ignored. The wild thing—Lila—is taken in, is saved, as completely as Marilynne Robinson knows how to save her, with love and community, becoming a preacher's wife and a mother, living inside the preacher's spiritual house, which is very unconfining. He is keen to the mystery of the nothing we know about anything, but he is convinced of a final or ultimate or original goodness or benevolence which he has domesticated into a neighborly god because it is comforting and useful to do that, if also comical.

Lila is baptized like other savages the world over, understanding hardly a speck of what's going on, but sensing an improvement of circumstances. The preacher knows that. Maybe really that's the very thing that has allowed her to unlock his locked life of faith and good works and examinations of conscience; she is a breath of fresh air. She has no assumptions he shares. He can in a way be reborn, before language, as much as he wants to be, in Lila. She doesn't know what to expect of anyone or anything beyond being run off. The preacher, on the other hand, was born into a line of preachers.

So Marilynne Robinson has dropped two extremes into one box and lets them have at it. I don't wind up at all sure that Lila will stay in Gilead once the old preacher (I should be saying reverend) dies, even though it seems like all she could do, since she has the boy and he won't be wild-hearted like Lila. But Robinson has—as always—kept the cosmos open in her book. She's apparently interested in Calvin's god, whatever that would mean, but it must be a very big god that doesn't hold her back from wandering us out to the last dots on a disk of snow.

III

On a Poem by Hopkins

Spring and Fall

to a young child

Margaret, are you grieving
Over Goldengrove unleaving?
Leaves, like the things of man, you
With your fresh thoughts care for, can you?
Ah! as the heart grows older
It will come to such sights colder
By and by, nor spare a sigh
Though worlds of wanwood leafmeal lie;
And yet you *will* weep and know why.
Now no matter, child, the name:
Sorrow's springs are the same.
Nor mouth had, no nor mind, expressed
What heart heard of, ghost guessed:
It is the blight man was born for,
It is Margaret you mourn for.

As with so much Hopkins, this poem is preposterously beautiful. Its difficult syntax compels its reader to submit to its world almost immediately. Well, even *before* we get to the improbable "man, you—can you?" the neologisms have altered our minds: "Goldengrove unleaving." I don't know if Goldengrove is an actual stand of deciduous trees or not; I vote for Hopkins having invented this tract name to carry all the beauty of loss in a single word. Hear the sounds of "go, go" in G*o*lden*gr*ove; simply to invoke a golden grove is to say it is *going.* The poem reminds me of Frost's "Nothing Gold Can Stay"—both poems so immense and sad to the point of peace. There is no escape from loss—unless the pure beauty of the poems provides one, as it does for me.

But back to "unleaving." The new word is generated, I would imagine, by the unstudied opening line, "Margaret, are you *grieving*?" That's something Hopkins might have written quickly, and it would have given him—always ready to forge new words—the rhyming word "unleaving," which of course just means ordinary losing-its-leaves, and is a convenience. But it also happens to operate as a pun on leaving's other sense—going away. Here it is *un*leaving, of course, but the "leave," like the "go" in Goldengrove, is planted in our mind's ear.

This couplet, "Margaret, are you grieving / Over Goldengrove unleaving?" is as easy on the tongue as the following couplet is impossible: "Leaves, like the things of man, you / With your fresh thoughts care for, can you?" Let me just say that my hat is *off* to Hopkins for this. I've never really examined this poem before, having submitted to it utterly at the age of nineteen. This is the point at which Hopkins compels us to take off our clothes and enter his river. It is wildly strained, forced, manipulated, and—we already feel—worth it. *If we are not compelled to submit in some way to a poem it cannot change us.* That makes perfect sense, now that I've written it, but I don't think I ever thought of it before. So this is not a tormented couplet that we forgive for the greater good of the poem, averting our eyes discreetly from that howler, "man, you—can you?"; this is the couplet of our entrance, of our acceptance of Hopkins's terms. He can continue from here. He has made aesthetic decisions so aggressive—the "you" after "man" hanging at the end of line three; the postponement of "can you" (with the help of lots of commas) to the end of line four—which just in sorting out the sense sends the mind rummaging back through the couplet, while at the same time moving forward. We're converts here, or we've quit.

But let me pause at the pair of words "fresh thoughts" referring to the grieving Margaret. Hopkins is surprised at Margaret's grief at the falling of the leaves of Goldengrove. How can she care for them, or for "the things of man"? Aren't we at some *early* point immune to the knowledge of loss? I wonder if the little prick of added sadness when Hopkins *sees* that Margaret is *not* immune wasn't itself what provoked this fifteen-line poem dropping all the leaves in the world.

It is so interesting how the first few lines of a poem do the hard work. We are now prepared for the development of the feeling of *division* in these next two couplets. First, division within the self—that is, Hopkins's own loss of his *original* knowledge of loss, which always comes in a specific circumstance, as it has for Margaret seeing Goldengrove unleaving. Hopkins feels the separation of his child self from his older self. I feel, although I don't see exactly what's doing it, something like the pain of cell division, with its strange stretching and weird afflictions.

A chill and distance enter lines five to eight. You will grow accustomed to things like this, the lines say. By now we are used to the rhymes, the syntactical inversions (worlds of wanwood *leafmeal lie*) and the new words he's created. The compressions of two words into one—wanwood; leafmeal—don't cause a ripple; they're perfect for something that makes natural and emotional sense to us. Wanwood: vivid *Golden*groves reduced to colorlessness; and the knowledge arrives on the little blowing-out *w*'s—*w*orlds of *w*an*w*ood—the color is blown off. Leafmeal: no longer leaves, just as no longer golden. The leaves are ground to meal. They aren't crisp and rattly and gold; they are a pale paste. We see this in crushed leaves, how they go grey, how they are undone. And in ourselves, how brightness is so bafflingly lost and how *edgeless* (*worlds* of wanwood) the diminishment is.

Here in line nine is the turn of this not-sonnet: "And yet you will weep and know why." Now the separation of Hopkins from the young girl is reversed. Hopkins *embraces* her (and with her, his own child self) as he inducts her into the endlessness, the bottomless-ness of loss. It is magnificently beautiful, the *oneness* Hopkins paradoxically generates among all of us in describing how we will lose one another. Here is the lesson: You're not wrong to weep, and "*will* weep." All sorrow comes from the same spring.

Now comes the achievement of the unachievable when Hopkins's syntax goes all squirrely with the "nor, no, nor" thing. This is *useful*, I would even say *necessary*, this incomprehensibility of the grammar. We *do* read it, and we are moved out of our grammar into something that could be spiritual if there were a spirit beyond this readiness to know the spiritual. But the great openness generated by these strange words is absolutely *smacked*; there is nothing to receive the spiritual vulnerability. This is emphatically not a Christian poem; it is as dark as Frost. All that our greatest sensors, our farthest probes, are met with is in the final couplet: "It is the blight man was born for, / It is Margaret you mourn for." The world "blight" is a thrilling achievement. It incinerates, it blackens, it *curses* and damns. All will die, and there is no consolation. You are mourning for yourself, and when I say you, Margaret, I mean me (says Hopkins). See how Hopkins has increased the *tenderness* in this lesson: "Now no matter, *child*, the name." His voice is holding us tenderly to him, instructing us: he bewitches us with the sorcery of "nor," "no," "nor," then he clubs us with "blight." If the word had been, say, "fate"—"It is the *fate* man was born for"—I think the whole poem would collapse. It is the word "blight"—absolute, harsh, and *natural*; a natural evil, something that wipes out what was living—that charges the poem backwards.

And that is one of the particular beauties of poetry as opposed to, say, the novel. A poem really has no beginning and end, although it does appear to. All the parts of a poem exist as a sort of plasma, simultaneously apprehended, existing in the mind all at once, as soon as we have become familiar with them. The word "blight" constantly and forever charges every word in the poem, shores every word in the poem. It is Indra's net, everywhere is the center, reflecting all. This great capacity of poetry is seldom so well exercised as it is here. The fact that the mind can move around in a poem—is asked to do this—is why poetry is considered the supreme art. Poetry is the shape and size of the mind. It works the *way* the mind works. It is deeply *compatible* with whatever it is we are. We dissolve in it; it dissolves in us.

This poem, "Spring and Fall," has reminded me of why I want to continue to try to write poems. I am grateful to it.

Postscript

In such great poems, there is always so much more left to say when you have said what you thought you wanted to say. Now I am thinking of Hopkins's beginning and

ending with "Margaret" and the great transformation
of what we come to understand to be Margaret. At the
beginning, Margaret is a child, seeing something sad,
addressed by an older person. She is discrete, separate.
By the end it is difficult to express all that Margaret is:
she is still *one*—one person, who will die, one person
who must suffer the knowledge that all will be lost
and she will lose herself. And yet it is this retention of
Margaret's identity by name that creates the greatest
poignancy: not, Hopkins could have said, *all* will be lost,
but *Margaret* will be lost. In keeping it singular in this
way each *single* living thing is a jewel in Indra's net. Each
self contains the universe. Each *self* must experience its
extinction. Each self is tender toward itself. Hopkins is
Margaret. We are Margaret; the unassuageable grief is
not that we will all die but that *Margaret* will die with
the knowledge that there are only Margarets . . . some
of whom are so young they don't yet know.

Radiantly Indefensible

1.

The central thing I want to think about is the mystery of—I want to call it *profundity*, which seems all wrong for Stevie Smith. But impact seems inadequate.

No, it *is* inadequate; impact just means that one is struck; profundity means that when one is struck, one sees deep stars. So profundity.

Stevie Smith's poetry had a profound impact on me, how about that.

I was looking for Stevie Smith, so hard. I turned over libraries and bookstores for years, trying to find her. I didn't know her name or anything about her; I didn't know what country she came from or what kind of poetry she would write or that it would have little drawings.

All I could find was not-her. I would find a piece of something here and another one there, but they couldn't be put together. I mean, in the living; there was always plenty to adore among the immortals. But anybody alive. I was young, and I thought there must be someone; now I wouldn't assume that. We are occupying such a thin wedge of time, what are the chances?

It seems so unfair, how the heart is. Why couldn't I feel the same about Auden? Surely Auden is profound and so wise and weary and puckish too, obviously a vastly more elastic soul and mind and talent. Or Larkin. Larkin was alive then, when Stevie Smith was, in the seventies. Maybe I didn't know about Larkin then. But even if I had known, it would have been like Auden, or like Frost. I would tug at my forelock (for even then I had a forelock).

It must be said, it appears, that reverence has its limits as a useful feeling. I never felt my hand going up to my forelock when I read Stevie Smith, even the first time, standing up in City Lights. It was so wonderful to have the thing in my hands at last, a white paperback with a scribbled drawing of the head of a girl on the cover, as it turned out. I had expected that however it would look, the book I was looking for, it would be unprepossessing on the outside, but even at that. It looked fey. Not that I paid it any attention then, or really ever, when I think about it. Fey is something we get less and less amused by the older we get; if it isn't a pose it's a kind of stunting, one no better than the other.

2.

"Duty was his Lodestar"
a song

Duty was my Lobster, my Lobster was she,
And when I walked with my Lobster
I was happy.

But one day my Lobster and I fell out,
And we did nothing but
Rave and shout.

Rejoice, rejoice, Hallelujah, drink the flowing champagne,
For my darling Lobster and I
Are friends again.

Rejoice, rejoice, drink the flowing Champagne-cup,
My Lobster and I have made it up.

I can hardly begin to suggest the courage this poem gives to me. The strength of character it takes to set down something so radiantly indefensible.

I must suppose "Duty was his Lodestar" is an inspirational song that British people would recognize, but I don't know anything about it. Which means I'm not even *getting* this spoof the way SS would have intended.

But as soon as she changed Lodestar to Lobster she had me. My friend Genie just sent me a *New Yorker* cartoon of a bunch of geese flying in formation, one wearing a propeller hat. The next goose turns to him and says, "That stopped being funny a thousand miles ago."

I'm with the goose in the propeller hat. Jokes have real staying power in my book.

It gives me so much hope, to see language get pantsed.

It's one thing to have duty as a lodestar: a high-toned piety one might repeat: perfect for lip service.

It's another thing to have duty as a lobster. It doesn't work at all. It just won't abstract right. The lobster has torn free of duty by the first line. What we get is a clattery lobster dance with breaking-up and making-up.

In fact, we might say—it has just occurred to me— that the joy of this poem is that *it* has torn free of duty. The duty to be more than a prank, duty to rhyme decently, to keep to a rhythm, to find fresh words even.

It's the special fun of laughing someplace you're not supposed to laugh, like church. Because it must be said that the fun results from scrambling the piety; the fun is had at the expense of sobriety. And it wouldn't be much fun to think about the lobster if one were *not* thinking about its not being a lodestar.

Maybe this poem really only works for people who are tyrannized by duty.

3.

> *It's a strange courage you lend me, ancient star . . .*
> *. . . . . toward which you lend no light.*

This is a snatch of Williams I have loved. I don't know if I even have this part right.

How weirdly little it takes, how few words.

It's almost discouraging it's so powerful.

Why do we write so much?

A few words of it do the job.

It's not that I'm less lonely thanks to it. It's access to the great hall of loneliness, the Milky Way. Williams is out here. It feels good to have company.

But what I wanted to do was to apply this line to the Stevie Smith "Duty" poem.

Her poem gives me that strange courage.

All I trust is whistling in the dark.

Borges thought there were maybe seven metaphors, everything resolved into those seven.

Something like that.

I guess the big job is trying to hold off the rush of matter toward itself, the collapse of space.

And of course the collapse of time. The "Sweet Afton" thing.

Poetry is generative—the tiniest bit of it—it's like an Alka-Seltzer disk bubbling, creating a ridiculous abundance of someplace else.

There is a permanent time that poetry lets us into. There are doors in all the centuries, feeding into this permanent time.

Bronk talks about this in relation to the stonework of Machu Picchu; there is work that enters another kind of time.

Because poetry isn't *it*, it isn't a thing, it's the *portal*.

But that's also funny because poetry *is* the thing.
I love the picture of the pointing finger: I love to
study it. I don't even care what it's pointing toward.
I don't look where the finger instructs me to look. I
look at the finger.

Or let me say rather, it is entirely insufficient that the
finger is pointing to something. It depends upon the
quality of the picture of the finger. So what if some
poorly made thing is pointing to the Milky Way?

I haven't got this at all well yet.

Exact articulation is all there is.

Something exactly right is the door through itself.

So it matters utterly.

But here's the thing: the thing that's exactly right
may be a tiny part of a great deal that is much less
exact, not very right at all and certainly not *that*
right. Actually it's got to be like that. Almost everything has to be packaging material. The job of almost
all the words is to suspend the essential words, which
cannot exist without some context.

This is ennobling all the way around. It imparts value
to all the whistling needed to suspend those two
transcendent notes that open the dark.

Nor will you know in advance which will be the
two notes and which the packing.

All Love All Beauty

Dublinesque

Down stucco sidestreets,
Where light is pewter
And afternoon mist
Brings lights on in shops
Above race-guides and rosaries,
A funeral passes.

The hearse is ahead,
But after there follows
A troop of streetwalkers
In wide flowered hats,
Leg-of-mutton sleeves,
And ankle-length dresses.

There is an air of great friendliness,
As if they were honouring
One they were fond of;
Some caper a few steps,
Skirts held skilfully
(Someone claps time),

And of great sadness also.
As they wend away
A voice is heard singing
Of Kitty, or Katy,
As if the name meant once
All love, all beauty.

—*Philip Larkin*

This poem sends feeling down a narrow channel, and you don't even know it's feeling until it explodes in a delicious mist at the end. It looks like a lot of scenery, local Dublin color, first the "sidestreets" with their "pewter" light from the "afternoon mist" that causes the lights to be on in the pokey shops of a particularly stock-Irish description "above race-guides and rosaries." Larkin's art is on intensely quiet display: so much atmosphere is generated in so few words. It's grey, it's low, it's mean, it's tight, and something is *coming*. Nice to start with that preposition, "*Down* stucco sidestreets." Each element moves into the next: street>light>mist>light bulbs hanging over "race-guides and rosaries." It feels cozy, damped down, dim. A channel, but for what? Larkin is so good at creating motion in a poem.

A funeral! This is a tiny poem, so all of this happens before it registers. But if one were to anticipate what kind of funeral this would turn out to be, you'd expect it to be . . . narrow and grey. Which is just what it isn't. It's loose and colorful, filled with warmth and exchanges, capers, clapping, song: "A troop of streetwalkers . . . honouring / One they were fond of." Larkin gives us their dress, which feels so flowery and flouncy and animated, the opposite of the narrow street—"wide flowered hats, / Leg-of-mutton sleeves, / And ankle-length dresses." Consider this attention to dress which sounds anachronistic even for the time. These women sound like Miss Kitty from *Gunsmoke*, attractive like that. And there's a gang of them, they are their own self-approving community, progressing down the streets after the hearse, flamboyantly what they are, warm, united, and sad.

The poem moves to the interior so seamlessly. The static streets are invaded—the Dublin mist is rent—by this gaudy funeral. First the women's clothes, then their women's capers. Things are getting more and more animated. The poem brims with warmth by the end of stanza three and stanza four brings it home through a single exquisitely baffled detail, a specific so specific that it becomes unspecific: are they singing of "Kitty, or Katy"?

This stanza is a marvel. First notice how cinematic it is. This whole poem has been movielike; the passage of the procession into and then out of the frame of the poem.

In this last stanza we don't see them at all, just the disembodied voice "heard singing," just the trailing voice raised in song. That means we have come to Larkin's real stage, always: the pure interior. This place tends to be troubled when he gets there, but in "Dublinesque" it is incredibly sweet. Maybe because Larkin has watched like a camera, he hasn't got his usual gloom spiral going. It's a sound camera, and doesn't quite catch the name: Kitty, or Katy. And now the relaxation of this camera discipline: "As if the name meant once / All love, all beauty."

Enough cannot be said about this ending. Let me point out first the parallels in the rhythm and single instance in the poem of rhyme: of Kitty, or Katy / all love, all beauty.

The unrhymed poem ends, then, with a rhyme, and it opens on two of the great themes in all poetry: love and beauty. It invokes *all* love, *all* beauty. And guess what? It works; we feel the tide.

Because Larkin has succeeded in narrowing the opening to the point of blur. Kitty *or* Katy. This is so specific to this Dublin moment that it isn't at all specific. Exact identity is lost as love and beauty are lost except absolutely available at the same fuzzy moment. First Larkin goes to the trouble to create a rich moving picture; then he erases it, or at least erases the object of it, Kitty or Katy, then he claps on the two biggest abstractions in English poetry: love and beauty. And it works like a charm.

This is one of those moments when everything coalesces. Everything is available because everything's gone: no one is there; the street is empty.

I want to think about the genius of "Kitty, or Katy." Everything depends upon this dislocation, this paradoxical exact focus of all love, all beauty.

It's an exact focus that can't find its mark and is therefore slippery and silky word-mist. The focus is baffled and ramified; it's tiny. We don't know if it's Kitty or Katy and we can't settle. Now Larkin can dump whatever he wants into us because we are between places; that's exactly where we are: between. It's perfect for poetry which has to get into the cracks, has to find and work the cracks. There has to be some way to let in the dazzle, to perfume the works.

This poem succeeds because it's short and brisk; the deep dwelling occurs at parade speed. The parade of bright flowery streetwalkers becomes a gesture, taken all together, a single surprise flowery sweep across pewter. They are the same gesture that Frost's crow makes in knocking snow onto Frost and giving his heart a change of mood. They bring a gift, then; they change the poet. Larkin is left in the street with the fumes of all love, all beauty.

On a Poem by Dickinson

#372

I know lives, I could miss
Without a Misery—
Others—whose instant's wanting—
Would be Eternity—

The last—a scanty Number—
'Twould scarcely fill a Two—
The first—a Gnat's Horizon
Could easily outgrow—

A tidy little poem, but nothing too special if you just take the first four of its eight lines. They're pretty predictable Emily Dickinson—some people she wouldn't mind missing, while the loss of others would immediately feel like eternity. It's wonderful to think that this is just standard ED, how her mind cannot help generating instant opposites and categories and how she goes on to find little pleasures inside them such as the sound pun of "lives, I could *miss* / Without a *Mis*ery" or the compression of an "instant's wanting." "Eternity" is always at hand for her poetic deployment but in this case it exerts no particular force.

It's the second quatrain that makes the poem sit up. In it she goes back to revisit the categories of the first stanza (as she often does). Those she'd miss would "scarcely fill a Two," making the two a container, like a measuring cup, say—a very strange amount of *person*, obviously—a pleasing abstraction into some absolute fluid. She is summary; she is absolute; she is vigorously exercising her discriminatory powers; she is having fun.

Then in the last two lines she has more fun, and that fun is her intention here has to gradually dawn on the reader. The lives she wouldn't mind missing are *so* many that "a Gnat's Horizon / Could easily outgrow." Now a gnat, being the emblem of tininess, enjoys the largest possible horizon since it occupies the least possible space. Thus the people ED doesn't care about are more than all space minus a gnat. Thus they verge on *all space*, growing all the time. She is wonderfully dismissive, enlivened by the negative pole of her very polar soul.

No one else could possibly have written this poem. It is so amused, so effortlessly, uniquely cockeyed. Note the tightening focus of the second quatrain: how it has locked down on those generalizations as on a microscope slide.

She would be sitting there—first just thinking about how so few people really matter (not even a big enough number to admit her small family, you note) and how so many *don't* matter. Then her image-maker starts up. The "fill a Two" seems easy till you think of it—it's just about impossible to stay that close to the abstraction of *naming* a number (two) and making it physical. She does this with the absolute economy of a single verb: "fill." Now a two is a thing, a container, here not quite topped up, a slightly underfilled two-tank.

The more I think about this "two," the more I admire it. It takes almost no work to slide into the reader's understanding. The "Gnat's Horizon," on the other hand, while probably affording her more fun to think up, takes a little more work on our part, making it a little strained and thus inferior.

The sounds of the poem are agreeable and easy to say. The rhymish bits—Misery / Eternity; Two / grow—add a mild glue to a fine little morning's work.

No Time for Anything
but Repetition

Tichborne's Elegy

WRITTEN WITH HIS OWN HAND IN THE TOWER
BEFORE HIS EXECUTION

My prime of youth is but a frost of cares;
My feast of joy is but a dish of pain,
My crop of corn is but a field of tares,
And all my good is but vain hope of gain:
The day is past, and yet I saw no sun,
And now I live, and now my life is done.

My tale was heard, and yet it was not told,
My fruit is fallen, and yet my leaves are green,
My youth is spent, and yet I am not old,
I saw the world, and yet I was not seen:
My thread is cut, and yet it was not spun,
And now I live, and now my life is done.

I sought my death, and found it in my womb,
I looked for life, and saw it was a shade,
I trod the earth, and knew it was my tomb,
And now I die, and now I was but made;
The glass is full, and now the glass is run,
And now I live, and now my life is done.
                    —*Chidiock Tichborne* (1586)

Look at the good it does a man to know he will be hanged in the morning. He has no time for anything but repetition. This is an eighteen-line poem of a single pure shocked bafflement said sixteen ways (he repeats one way three times). He knows two mutually exclusive things directly on top of each other. The lines should all be read at the same time; even the half-lines should be stacked on top of each other and read at once; maybe every word—all the words at once—to get at the simultaneity. There is something that can neither be digested nor got beyond: now I *live*, and now my life is *done*.

Tichborne goes over and over it, running through a lifetime's worth of metaphors for loss. And since this *is* his whole lifetime, why not?

Metaphor can take the weight of this; it holds; not a drop of loss has been lost in five centuries. When you have no time, when something has to last, trust a stack of metaphors.

The End of the Party

I had been reading the Saturday *New York Times* and came to the obituaries, which I always hope to enjoy. In a short graceful obituary for a woman of a certain age with a good haircut (photo) was quoted, by her daughter I assume, a poem that had made the dead woman cry. It turned out to be a poem by Philip Larkin. (One is always braced for the worst.) The grace of the whole thing, the pleasure in seeing this Larkin poem that ran in the *New Yorker* a couple years ago—something he never published, but nonetheless worthy—made me feel a number of things.

One, I wished I sought out excellence and beauty more and spent less time on maddeningly unnourishing newspapers.

Two, the experience reinforced my conviction that what moves me, jars me, cannot be sought but must surprise me. It must always come and save me. So I don't have to worry about spending too much time on newspapers.

Three, the wonderful power of this Larkin poem comes clearly and simply from its being exactly what Larkin would write, from its issuing from a single self. It is his envy of those who can live forward, his chronic sense of missing out, and his enviable technique. But the stamp of him is the thing, how drenched in him the poem is and how that paradoxically gives the whole thing to us as readers. In feeling out his own exact sensation on that late-summer late afternoon and presenting it to us in its own atmosphere (not thinking he can say it, but only make something that might contain it) Larkin releases us to feel the moment from a variety of points of view. It seems clear that the dead woman had read the poem from the point of view of the woman Larkin is addressing, who has such an appetite for the future. That's wonderful to me. "She cried when she showed me this because it described the life she felt so lucky to have."

> We Met at the End of the Party
> We met at the end of the party
> When most of the drinks were dead
> And all the glasses dirty:
> "Have this that's left," you said.
> We walked through the last of summer
> When shadows reached long and blue

Across days that were growing shorter:
You said, "There's autumn too."
Always for you what's finished
Is nothing, and what survives
Cancels the failed, the famished,
As if we had fresh lives
From that night on, and just living
Could make me unaware
Of June, and the guests arriving,
And I not there.

Or perhaps I underestimate the dead woman, and she felt the whole thing.

But look how a poem, the presence of this Larkin poem, opens a contemplative space in the air, how it releases the newspaper reader from doom and emergency (the failed and famished) into some kind of suspension and balance of forces.

Really, we have here regular old Larkin, morose, losing out, fearing death, and *using* that exact stuff: he has appointed a poem with furniture so right, and just enough of it, that we can move around forever sensing a symphony all around us.

All the Nothing

1.

> Oh
> the sumac died
> it's
> the first time
> I
> noticed it

Why in the world should that give me the lift it does?

Well, it has nothing to do with Williams's larger intentions for it as an illustration of "American Idiom and the Variable Foot," which I have never found very interesting. For me, it has exactly to do with thinking of it as the whole thing, not a little bit of something longer.

Things inside other things have to take their place, jockey for position, exist in relation. With long strings of things, one thing must fade that another can brighten;

the eye moves on. It's the built-in sorrow of serial attention, enfilades mowed down.

Taken alone, these lines keep their brain shock, which
mimics the shock of first noticing something outside us.
Our attention is complete and undivided. We notice, say,
that the sumac—which would have taken some extended
period of time to die—has died. So at the same time that
the brain is acknowledging that the sumac is dead it is
compressing the whole (lost) narrative of its getting dead.

To acknowledge something new is to be engaged
in catch-up; the mind rewrites with impossible speed
what's been going on. The way this defies time matches
how creation works; Mozart apparently composed con-
certi in an instant; something that would have to be
played out in time took him no time; all the notes were
stacked right on top of each other. It's impossible and
true at the same time.

So it's all the nothing around the dancy little
arrangement of regular English that does it all the good.
All that nothing is what allows the mind to focus. All
the nothing gives the mind the gift of Just This, the
paradoxical vacation of perfect attention. Because it is
vacationlike to actually pay attention. Your world is
relieved of clutter for a split second. You collect like a

snowflake around this single bit of informational grit: Oh, the sumac died it's the first time I noticed it.

It looks like a poem about a sumac and death but it's a poem about the mind and the fresh slap of perception. Or rather, it isn't *about* perception, it gives us a pleasant tiny slap of it.

2.

How much can you take away? It's always a question. Or maybe it's exactly the wrong question, posed like that. If you think you are taking *away*, then you probably *are*—diminishing something. You have to be looking *for* something, feeling for the contours of the thing inside the distractions, trying to add just a little bit *more* to what you know.

But it's interesting to see what happens, just through the process of isolation. Isolation is a very simple form of "taking away." You don't simplify, say, the salt shaker by taking away its details; you take the regular salt shaker away from its kitchen and set it alone against white. You abstract it.

Things taken alone are instantly strange and liberated from usefulness. This doesn't cause the mind to perceive the salt shaker separate from relationships, since the only way the mind knows anything is through relationships, but it changes the points of the relationship; the mind is incited to hook it up by different points, to connect the salt shaker to itself (the mind seeks to possess) in ways that seem aesthetic because the aesthetic is the not-useful, the beautiful. Removing something from usefulness also removes it from time, suspending it in the white time of the mind.

So when Williams abstracts a single observation—Oh, the sumac died—the result is predictably paradoxical. It looks like it matters that it's a sumac, but because of this extreme detachment, the way *one* thing has been cut out of the fabric of life and isolated, specificity works in a different way from usual. It doesn't matter at all that it's a sumac.

The poem has worked the way the brain works when it suddenly knows: it is thoroughly focused on the new thing to the exclusion of all else; it knows with inexplicable suddenness (after having *not* known) and it backfills the story.

Because this little poem is about how we perceive: the brain *suddenly* knows that the sumac is dead. In a split second it recovers the event it was oblivious to. It knows what it missed. Dying is a process, but in this poem we come in at the end so the process occurs backwards.

It's a jolly poem about the slap of fresh knowledge, any knowledge. So what if it's death here. It flushes the mind.

Listening to Williams

Listening to this old recording of William Carlos Williams reading at the 92nd Street Y made me think again about the whole question of voice and where it resides: is it on the stage or on the page? I must confess a predisposition to the page.

Certainly when you read Williams on the page it feels like you're hearing him. As Kenneth Rexroth says, "his poetic line is organically welded to the American speech like muscle to bone."

But what that means is, this sense of American speech—of language on the streets—is coming from things Williams is doing *on the page*. Much of the power, for example, comes from the loose, staggered arrangement of his lines, the kind of air and scatter it catches.

The poems feel blown around. Some of my favorites have nearly been blown away. We sense this terrific freshness and immediacy when we read Williams; we hear this arrestingly authentic, direct voice. It's such an interesting paradox: we can *see* a *voice*; we *hear* through the *eyes*. But I think that's the way it is, really, with poetry: I think poetry's voice happens in the reader's head. The voice need never pass over anybody's actual physical vocal chords. I could imagine that some of Emily Dickinson's poems were never said aloud. And come to think of it, what voice could be their mental equal? The best poet's best voice is never transmissible outside of individual skulls, and that's fine by me. The poet speaks to one reader at a time, forever.

And here's a further mystery to ponder: the language in Williams's poems *feels* authentic, wicked straight up from the pool of mid-twentieth-century American life. But if that were really so, the language would be dated in the way that DeSotos are dated; it would just be interesting for collectors.

But that isn't the case; poetry draws from its time, absorbs and uses the available language, but it does something to it, something that takes the ephemeral out of it. Since that's its job: it has to last. It's a spectacular trick: lasting poetry, in some more lasting way than ephemeral speech, sounds like ephemeral speech. You can test this, even in translation. Catullus is always shockingly bright and immediately alive across languages, giving us the sense of the ephemeral.

As a young reader, I was bewitched by how Williams's poems relish the interstices and make no place more vivid. And how they do this by doing almost nothing:

Between Walls

the back wings
of the

hospital where
nothing

will grow lie
cinders

in which shine
the broken

pieces of a green
bottle

It seems utterly obvious that we have to *read* a poem like this; it is nothing spoken.

It's the lines on the page that put the air in it and Williams's excisions of words and punctuation that relieve it of gravity. If we were to hear Williams's voice, it would be in the way of Williams's voice.

Still, I wind up interested, and grateful, for the recording. We sense his years and his sweetness, his irrepressible enthusiasm, his desire to connect with people, his lack of a defensive or polished surface. And we hear the clear warmth of the 92nd Street Y's audience in response. It would have been a pleasure to be there that night, in the physical presence of a modern master.

But—I despair of his delivery. He mangles his poems, hesitating, clustering phrases oddly, faking emphasis as though certain words had been <u>underlined!</u> and he had to <u>really!</u> say those <u>loudly!</u> He robs them of their lightness and their gravity. He runs over them in his car.

But fortunately they are written on paper, and there they go right back to full vitality, as he himself has presciently described in his lovely poem "The Term":

The Term

A rumpled sheet
of brown paper
about the length

and apparent bulk
of a man was
rolling with the

wind slowly over
and over in
the street as

a car drove down
upon it and
crushed it to

the ground. Unlike
a man it rose
again rolling

with the wind over
and over to be as
it was before.

Con and Pro

1. Walt Whitman

I have promised myself not to go back and look into Whitman or I'd be cheating, since I'm supposed to be writing about a writer I don't read. Also, if I did I know that I would be undone, drawn in, persuaded. That is one of the problems with reading great writing: you can lose sight of the fact that you really don't like it. It takes a long time to retrieve yourself. I feel that it is essential to operate exclusively on prejudice here.

I guess I could say I don't read Whitman because I don't need Whitman's big stride, his wide, encompassing arms, his hug. The poets I go back to are not at all welcoming. I don't apparently like to be welcomed. My poets are a dryish people. Lonely, and what of it. They do not gather round the campfire. My poets don't cherish even the illusion of ease and camaraderie; they do not laze and invite their souls; their souls are much too aggressive already. What their souls need is a little discipline, thank you.

We may make our choices about what poets we continue to read according to how we're attracted to their body type. Body of work, that is. When I think of Whitman I think of bulk. Page after page of the *same poem*, rectangle after ripe rectangle of self-delighted self-examination, undulating in the hot wholesome American breeze like sections of Kansas wheat. There is a chain of stores in the Sacramento area whose name translates this agricultural metaphor of numbing abundance into today's urban landscape: Big Lots!, the chain is called.

I like skinny-bodied poets, the stringy ones who don't impress the boys on the poetry beach. Nobody is tempted to take steroids and pump up their own poetry mass after they read these poets' work. Let's admit it, Whitman just begs to be followed: whatever is true of me is true of you also, dooming us to an ever-broadening band of self-fascinated brothers, even if some are sisters.

To my mind, poets should discourage the practice of poetry, by example. Poetry should seem hopelessly, inimitably beautiful, dependent upon a touch you'd have to be born with. And preferably it should pounce and clean your bones quickly, rather than boil you for three weeks the way Whitman does.

2. William Bronk

I love to open the big book of William Bronk poems, *Life Supports*, and read one at random. It doesn't matter which one shows up because they all release the same bracing smell and parch of stone, the same chill of stone in the shade. I don't remember a single individual Bronk poem, and I don't know if they're actually memorable; anyhow, they don't matter to me in that way. For me they're like the small brown bottle my grandmother carried in her purse and sniffed for the pick-me-up jolt.

However little you thought you'd been trafficking in surfaces and ornament, after a Bronk poem you realize it was much too much; however cleansed of illusions you believed yourself to be, it looks like they built up anyhow. Bronk takes them off like paint stripper. You're shriven, your head is shaved. The experience is religious in its ferocity and disdain for cheap solace.

Here, let me open to a poem—and I swear this
one just turned up:

The Effect of Cause Despaired

Wanting the significance that cause and effect
might have (we see it in little things where it is)
not seeing it in any place
important to us (it is in our lives but in ways

that deny each other) and the totality,
I suppose, is what I mean—it isn't there—
we look around: the possibilities,
dreams and diversions, whatever else there is.

If you aren't familiar with Bronk, maybe this doesn't
thrill you. But if you are, it's like dropping the needle
down into the endless groove of an implacable, insa-
tiable, relentless intelligence that allows itself not the
least shred of consolation, not the thinnest veil of pro-
tection. Bronk's poems are almost entirely abstract and
disembodied, as the poem above, his language desic-
cated but also conversationally halting and embedded.
There is no flesh, no world, precious little metaphor—as
though every human attachment is cheating. If anything
seems to work—such as cause and effect—it never adds

up to anything. "We look around," and, in the absence of any system that could explain our actions to ourselves, whatever "dream" or "diversion" we cook up is understood to be just that—a distraction from nothing.

Bronk is thinking and thinking, as purely as possible, about how we want—want not to be alone, want things to matter, want to feel that we are connected to reality. His poems are all about wanting and how there is no end to it. And about how whatever reality is, it is something we only know in the negative—by being constantly wrong about it.

Bronk's body of work is a strange achievement which it is hard not to call brave. There is such a grave honor in its repetitiveness, how it harps on what it can't have, and how it won't bend—can't bend. If I say that Bronk's poems are like blocks of stone, similar, but each slightly different and fitted one to another, and if I say that one experiences a strange exhilaration and release in the presence of the stark monument they form, then I am echoing Bronk's own description of the stonework of Machu Picchu in "An Algebra Among Cats," my favorite essay in his remarkable book of essays, *Vectors and Smoothable Curves*.

Bronk is compelled by the "plain perfection" of Machu Picchu's stones, whose "surfaces have been worked and smoothed to a degree just this side of that line where texture would be lost." Standing among them, he feels released from the idea of time as moving from past to future and the accompanying illusion of human progress: "It is at least as though there were several separate scales of time; it is even as though for certain achievements of great importance, this city for example, there were a continuing present which made those things always contemporary."

There are moments of aesthetic transport which weld beauty to beauty, occasional angles which offer a glimpse of something endless and compelling. Bronk feels it in the presence of the pure artifacts of Machu Picchu; I get a touch of it in the presence of Bronk.

IV

The Double

If I were only one person I could answer the question of how I perceive the audience for poetry in a single way. But I am two people, so I must answer in two ways—first, as the godlike writer of poems, serenely independent of Maslow's hierarchy of needs, and second, as her cousin.

1.

So to begin, let us draw close to the empyrean springs and ask the poet, even now dipping her alabaster hand into the poetical waters, how she feels about audience: "Do you think, as you write, about who will read your poems and how they will like them? Be honest."

No, I do not. My attention is entirely taken up by the voice in my head—a perfect tyrant, utterly without charity. And a pig for pleasure, I might add. Ordinary conditions do not obtain. Take the condition of time, for example. While I'm trying to satisfy this inside voice, time takes on that bulgy condition it has during the most critical stage of a skid, where astonishing maneuvers become possible simply because they must (or you'll crash). It is extremely occupying. When I was younger I noticed that I sweated terribly when I was writing, just as though it were very hard physical labor. I liked that evidence that I was grappling with something at least as difficult as uprooting an oak.

"You actually mean to say that you have no concern at all for any sort of reader?"

No, I cannot say that. There *is* a stain in the ichor— a sense of being watched and judged, and a desire for approval. When I am writing, I feel that I have insinuated myself at the long, long desk of the gods of literature— more like a trestle table, actually—so long that the gods (who are also eating, disputing, and whatnot, as well as writing) fade away in the distance according to the laws of Renaissance perspective. I am at the table of the gods and I want them to like me. There, I've said it. I want the great masters to enjoy what I write. The noble dead are my readers, and if what I write might jostle them a little, if there were a tiny bit of scooting and shifting along the benches, this would be my thrill. And I would add that the noble dead cannot be pleased with imitations of themselves; they are already quite full of themselves.

2.

On the other hand, the lofty condition enjoyed by the poet takes up only perhaps two hours, or 1/84, of a week. A *good* week. I must spend 83/84 of the week as my cousin.

This cousin has a higher and, I'm sorry to say, a lower nature. Her higher nature sees itself as the steward of the poet's work and responsible for helping that work secure a place in the world. This means that she must take an active, practical interest in living readers, not just by tidying poems themselves so that they're fit to be seen, but also by moving the poet's mover along the squares of the Poetry board the best she can. In this spirit, she seeks good journals for the poems and good presses for the books, accepts reading dates, and agrees to interviews, so that the poet might gain name recognition, by means of which the poet's poems might

reach an audience and rise or fall fairly, based upon
their merit, instead of simply resting upon the bottom
because nobody ever saw them.

On the other hand, the cousin's lower nature simply enjoys *la gloire*, which comes by way of the audience.
This spotlight hog trades eagerly upon the poems (which
she didn't write and only partially understands), larding
readings (the bigger the better) with comic remarks and
avoiding the poems that aren't snappy. She needs to
know the audience is out there, and the quickest way
to feel it is through their laughter. Her only ambition
is to hold the audience. I often see her as a betrayer of
the poet, but she isn't. Secretly they are best friends.

Reading before Breakfast

The books I regularly pick up in the morning, for the few minutes or half hour before I set about my own writing, are not casual interests. These are books I can *only* open in the morning because only *then* can I bear them. I go to these writers because they contain the original ichor. They are the potent Drink Me. On weak days, even a look at the blue, vertically striped spine of Joseph Brodsky's *Less Than One* or *On Grief and Reason* repels me.

My mother liked to tell how my brother as a little boy would sneak up on his Golden Book *Hansel and Gretel*, open it to the picture of the witch, and cry with fear. He came back again and again. My books are like that; I have reread them so often that they open to the witch.

I have two dozen morning books. Usually I can't remember when I read them for the first time. But sometimes I can; Nabokov's *Lectures on Literature* is the experience that endures from a long-ago camping trip to Lassen Volcanic National Park. It is dislocating to read a book of such aesthetic intensity out of doors; I'm not sure it's a good idea. The landscape twists tight as a tornado and vanishes, sucked down through the storm door of the book. There might be such a thing as too much torque. Instruments would record some very strange warping in that campground for those two or three days. Last summer a lovely bay on the Marin County coast was similarly sucked up, this time by Kundera's *Testaments Betrayed*.

In any case, reading is merely the first step to rereading. It has just occurred to me that rereading imitates our most picturesque images of creation and transformation. We have heard it reported, for example, that a whole concerto would come to Mozart in a single flash. A composition based on melody that must move through time—pages and pages of notation—arrives *stacked on top of itself*, or perhaps radiates out from some middle. Or, to offer a chemical analogy, imagine a glass filled with a supersaturated solution; if you give it a tap, it could turn to crystals. Rereading is like these mysteries. Open to a paragraph or even a line and—*tap!*—the complete composition precipitates. I never "acquire" these books. It is maddening, but I can never remember books, especially my favorite ones. I don't like them to come up in conversation. But if I reread a line, then it is all around me again, my real landscape, my real feelings, all familiar. *Where have I been?*

I often feel, along with the world at large, that we have quite enough poems. Writing a poem does not fit with much else in one's life. Except for the writing of poems, one might think of one's life as a busy restaurant that is pretty happy with itself. In order to write a poem I have to pass through that busy restaurant. This is where my books are critical. Those books are my goons. My goons go in first, pull out their guns, and clear the place. After that, I have my pick of tables; or I can just keep going.

First my books dispatch ordinary ideas of "community": "The essential thing that takes place between things does not take place through their intercourse, but through the seemingly isolated, seemingly unconcerned, seemingly unconnected action that each of them performs," says Martin Buber in his introduction to *The Legend of the Baal-Shem. Blam!* This kind of thinking gives a writer some elbow room.

Here one is free *not* to be oneself: "A book is the product of a *self other* than the self we manifest in our habits, in our social life, in our vices"; or "the writer's true self is manifested in his books *alone*." These are observations by Proust which Kundera quotes. Such quotes by my favorites offer a double joy. First, as in this instance, there is the attractiveness of what is quoted; and second, there is the pleasurable sensation of endless doors opening, author through author, all the way back to the first word. It is much bigger in here than in the restaurant.

One is freed of the oppression of "progress." Says William Bronk, admiring the unsurpassable beauty of Machu Picchu, "we have not advanced . . . as we have tried with the encumbrance of our far more numerous and varied skills to achieve a degree of perfection which was reached so simply here so long ago." I find it lovely to hear our skills acknowledged as "encumbrances." This comes from poet Bronk's book of essays, *Vectors and Smoothable Curves*. I notice that most of my morning books are by poets and novelists—but their essays rather than their poetry or novels. Naturally, since I choose them, my authors comment on each other and support certain attitudes—despising confession; quick to dispatch suffering ("Kafka did not *suffer* for us! He *enjoyed* himself for us!"—Kundera); bewitched by the "shimmer of the gratuitous" (Updike's introduction to Nabakov's *Lectures on Literature*). Here is Kundera augmenting Bronk on the subject of progress: "History is not necessarily a path climbing upward (toward the richer, more cultivated) . . . the demands of art may be counter to the demands of the moment (of this or that modernity), and . . . the new (the unique, the inimitable, the previously unsaid) might lie in some direction other than the one everybody sees as progress."

I cannot imagine that these snippets I am offering here are mixing the morning martinis in you that they are in me. Indeed, I hope they are not. I'm with Auden in *The Dyer's Hand*: "Occasionally I come across a book which I feel has been written especially for me and for me only. Like a jealous lover I don't want anybody else to hear of it." How can I say it? Such books are the private, the select company of a mind to which I often lack access myself.

To Be Miniature Is to Be Swallowed by a Miniature Whale

This is wisdom I gleaned from experience. And when I say gleaned I mean picked up off the ground after the commercial harvesters had come through. This is wisdom nobody much wanted; I surely didn't. Of course, much wisdom is things we never wanted to know. (Itself an additional piece of wisdom, again demonstrating how discouraging wisdom is.)

But to return to the question of the miniature, we find imbedded in this prescient line the design flaw inherent in the impulse to miniaturize: all in the world you wind up doing is changing the scale of everything. If you manage to make yourself small (I was thinking about trying to have a very small life to escape the interest of, say, fate), you only excite a small whale to swallow you.

The stories of the miniature go down and down and down; small becomes the new large, over and over. In *The Third Policeman*, the great Flann O'Brien gets the last chest the policeman makes so infinitesimally small that it took him "three years to make and it took . . . another year to believe [he] had." As with all processes, there is no end. The contemplation of the miniature is therefore destabilizing, dizzying, sickening. There isn't any size that's the "real size" after a while. (O'Brien could have gone on.)

I remember when Carol and I were riding our mountain bikes along the White Rim Trail in Utah for four days. To get down to the edge of the Colorado River where the trail was, we had to descend hundreds of feet of steep cliff. But then the trail was again at the edge of a steep cliff, below which toiled the muscular Colorado. After a bit of time we came to think of *our* level as ground level, and of the carved cliffs above us as mountains. Only at the end of the trip when we were again up top did we remember the "real" mountains that you see from up there.

Thinking, in general, so quickly becomes canyons inside canyons.

Of course, it is tempting to go where the great Walter Benjamin went, that is, adoring two grains of wheat with the whole *Shema Israel* inscribed on them because of their smallness, their compactness, how they embodied the most in the least space, and since the tiniest thing contains everything (Benjamin believed), the grains of wheat were the most excellent available token of that truth—though of course immense, crude, and partial by O'Brien's policeman's standards.

We *do* feel magic in certain small things. Perhaps because we imagine that operations in an unimaginably tiny dimension would work . . . better? . . . differently? In any case, by changing size, so that we can't get in there anymore, generating rooms too small to actually occupy, we give ourselves the possibility of everything turning out otherwise than it does *here*. We loosen an imaginative space that gets larger as it gets smaller.

All we're ever doing is messing with brain operations. Isolating such things is a fundamental ambition of the artist William Kentridge. He is fascinated with how art fools the eye and tries to isolate that place where the mind is both making a pattern and being patterned. He calls it a "membrane," in *Six Drawing Lessons*, the book of his Charles Eliot Norton Lectures. It can be drawing paper. It's any scrim that reveals the extreme vitality and flightiness of, what shall we call it, knowing?

A little poem is as fine a demonstration of this membrane as Kentridge's drawings of a black cat or rhinoceros or his scraps of black paper that can be scooted into an irresistible horse. We know the horse is scraps of paper and we also know—cannot resist knowing—that it is a horse. Not an "outside" horse, not a horse up on top of Utah on top of the White Rim Trail, but a magic horse. As the products of miniaturization are magic.

The poem occupies the same place; it is made partly by the poet (scooting words toward each other, words which may themselves be self-attractive) and partly by the reader when the mind cannot resist the horse. Employing the tastes of Walter Benjamin, I will argue that the poem that is closest to the size of two grains of wheat will hold the most magic.

And this is the magic I'm interested in: not the astonishment kind, not the how-did-he-*do*-that kind, but the release kind. You are not made to feel large and clumsy by comparison to the exquisite tiny thing; you are invited to eat the magic bean. You laugh. You feel . . . right-sized.

So the miniature: it can go two ways. It can make you kind of sick with its destabilization (the chest within

the chest within the chest, dimension called attention to
and forever unfixed, little becomes big becomes little).
Or it can make you feel kind of well with its destabilization: you find yourself comfortably inside of and just
the right size for someplace you can't be.

Against Influence

I've always bristled when it's been suggested that my work has been "influenced" by this or that poet. Sometimes the suggestion is laughably wrong—a poet I have never read let alone attempted to ventriloquize—and other times it's really true but no more useful than saying I'd been influenced by being a mammal. That is: true, but not distinguishing. Still, the question of influence remains an interesting one.

When I first became aware of the exhilarations of poetry as a community college freshman on the Mojave Desert, the poets who moved me were immaculately remote from my world. That was one of their attractions: Gerard Manley Hopkins, Jesuit priest, so incantatory I could barely understand him; John Donne, priest again, even earlier in the British lineage, and glorious crafter of something called *conceits*.

Lots of British priests in the poetry business, it
looked like. Plus Emily Dickinson. I loved the strenu-
ousness of it all, the rigors, the long lonely vigil of it,
the doomed quality. Here, I thought, is fit meat for the
mind. And the fact was that my mind was very hungry.

Hungry minds—the selfish, burrowing, opportunistic minds of the young who will rip the flesh off
anything that might feed them—these are the salvation
of writers. I often think about this, how the readers
who keep writing alive are comically self-serving; they
are trying to find access to their own brains, some way
in, some key to make their own heads work. They
rummage and plunder with catholic zeal, accidentally
performing a service to culture that no number of aca-
demics or disinterested readers could accomplish. They
have demonstrated one more time how great literature
keeps on freeing minds to do other things.

For me, pretty early, Frost worked. Not all of
him—I have never had the temperament for long
narratives—but it doesn't take much. Let us consider
the briefest of his lyrics.

Look at the nerve of this:

Dust of Snow

The way a crow
Shook down on me
The dust of snow
From a hemlock tree

Has given my heart
A change of mood
And saved some part
Of a day I had rued.

Frost has written this so limpidly that it would be possible to look right through it. That is, it would be possible to think that it was nothing special, instantly understandable and as quickly dismissed.

Stanza 1: A crow in a tree knocks snow down on the speaker.

Stanza 2: This tiny event shifts things inside the speaker.

Plus the poem rhymes: conventional rhymes in predictable places. Well, except maybe mood / rued.

This is just about the most exciting thing a poet can do: tread the edge of the banal. How close to nothing can he get and stay on the big side of nothing? Because the big side is really big. Borderless.

If we were to think of this little Frost poem as "conventional, predictable, dismissible," it would be something like Frost's own "day I had rued." That is, we would feel bored with it in advance of reading it, as Frost "rues" his day before he's finished it.

Except! Something dumps something on our head and we get that little Zen slap and it's all funny and broken up. We suddenly see that the conventions of the little poem, the predictability of crow/snow, heart/part, the whole little thing, is the thinnest shell around a mystery that we all know and that nevertheless remains a mystery: everything can shift at any instant. The poem does what the crow did. It cracks heads.

Frost is sneaky. While seeming to be quietly faithful to some quaint New England scene, he is actually stripping away every bit of extraneous color: the poem winds up as simple as a Japanese ink study. There is great energy available if you can stimulate the reader's conventional expectations and then hijack them. That's where the life always is, right as you walk under the tree expecting more New England and getting Japan instead.

The explosion of freedom inside the poem is pure neutral freedom, not named Frost or named anything;

it's denatured and become perfectly useful by an opposite temperament.

And this is what takes the onus off the idea of "influence." The thing that really sticks from a great poet like Frost isn't the snow and harness bells or the rest of it; it's the immense enduring enterprise of reclaiming freedom for himself poem by poem, how—like Hopkins or Donne or Dickinson—Frost was saving himself, and that saving always has a necessary dispatch—speed, impatience, relentlessness, stubbornness—that hooks it to all the other savings, until it's not influence at all but a shared ionized something.

On Forgetting

It is easy to be sentimental about memory because of its powers to intensify. If something is remembered, it has been selected by the mind, out of an almost infinite pool of things that might have been remembered but weren't. The thing remembered thus becomes important, simply *because* it has been remembered. How interesting is that? Who's to say that the unremembered silver fruit knife situated just behind the remembered peach wouldn't have made the better thing to have retained? This of course feels like a very unnatural argument; memories are important to us because we cannot control them—exactly because we cannot choose to remember the fruit knife rather than the peach. Memories seem to us like messages from the past whose author isn't quite the self we know. They have a position similar to dreams in the sense that they are visited upon us. They enjoy the respect and special lighting accorded the mysterious.

I suppose I have no quarrel with this, although I do think that people can get very stuck in detail if their memories are too accurate or, alternatively, they can live in an adolescent misty supercharged half-realm if their memories are *not* accurate but nonetheless *intense*, memories which have so ambered with repeated rememberings that they have become simplified, enlarged, and stylized (usually in the directions of Good and Evil).

But why am I talking about memory when I want to talk about forgetting. I have always had a memory especially defined by forgetting. It is hard to say, in my case, which is the cheese and which is the holes: I believe that emptiness (forgetting) may be the cheese, in which there are occasional suspended chambers of remembering.

If one has always been like this, it's not at all bad. In my case, I have been able to stand an incredible amount of routine because I'm not entirely aware that I have done it before. People with my sort of memory are good in positions requiring constant freshness in the face of what others might find unbearable repetition, the security guard's rounds, perhaps, or the toll taker's transactions. I should say here that lacking memory does not make one stupid; it could be argued that it makes one free. Of course this freedom can be frightening; one can be too untethered.

The great Borges respected forgetting and called it the dark side of the coin of memory. But I'm thinking now that he didn't go far enough. If on one side of the coin is memory, and on the other is forgetting, the coin's name can't be memory any more than the nickel's name is buffalo. Long ago there must have been a single name for this strange amalgam of memory and forgetting. It would have been silvery and velvety at once—quite impossible for modern tongues.

The Edges of Time

If a poem is going to be any good I have to write it before I feel I should, when I am still quite ignorant of its subject.

I undertook "The Edges of Time" with no more than a tiny vision of time as a physical substance, flattening out at the edges. But then things began to happen. Metaphors cropped up; rhymes wanted in. A kind of knowledge bred itself.

This is a very lucky thing for us. A poem can know more than we can know. It *must*. I suppose I should admit a secret about "The Edges of Time." It had the most banal origin. What got me thinking about the subject of time was my habit, long noted by my partner Carol, of suddenly having to do all kinds of things just when it was time for us to walk out the door to go someplace. Carol would stand there, keys in hand; *why* did I have to put away the dishes *now*? Couldn't I have done it earlier? No! I was stirred to action by *not* having time, by time's diminishment or thinning. It makes me laugh to think that a poem that I can now easily read as a meditation

on the approach of death—and which moves me because
Carol did become ill and did die, and both of us did
feel the "racket of claims" mentioned in the poem—was
written to explain why I couldn't get out the front door.
If I tried to write the poem now it would be too grave;
I would know too much; I could not.

The Edges of Time

It is at the edges
that time thins.
Time which had been
dense and viscous
as amber suspending
intentions like bees
unseizes them. A
humming begins,
apparently coming
from stacks of
put-off things or
just in back. A
racket of claims now,
as time flattens. A
glittering fan of things
competing to happen,
brilliant and urgent
as fish when seas
retreat.

The Poet Takes a Walk

This is actually an abstract walk, one I'm making up, a generalized walk based on what I like. I have usually done this on a bicycle, but I was asked to write about a walk, so I'll walk.

I'm walking along a road, not a busy road, a country road, but one where people do occasionally have things blow out of the back of their truck or their car window or even where people conceivably have *littered*. In any case, there are scraps of things here and there along the roadside. Bits of things, fragments of color and print, broken shapes, fading pink receipts.

There are whole things too, but I don't care about them. Except for a while I was very interested in the sheer phenomenon of the number of Styrofoam cooler lids I came across. In a way they were parts, in the sense that they were the top part of a cooler that wasn't any good anymore, going on down the road in the back of the truck. But I have never been especially interested in any story element in the things that lodge in the grasses in the inevitable ditch by the side of the road. I don't care if those people's beer gets hot. Well, of course I never want anybody's beer to get hot, but what I mean to say is that I'm not interested in the previous life of shards as they reveal things about people; I'm interested in the life *in* shards, among shards, between shards, shard-to-shard.

There are two related pleasures in studying roadside trash. One is identifying the whole from the part. A particular half-buried bit of orange cardboard can only be part of a Wheaties box. That greasy curve of flat black stuff has got to be from some kind of automotive gasket. I admire how good the mind is, what a small actual bit it needs to call up the whole, and how it attributes value to things simply because it recognizes them. I take the keenest pleasure in knowing that a small trapezoid of gold slashed with red is part of a Dos Equis label. I know it. I'm a weird expert in these identifications. I don't know how I trained, certainly not consciously. Maybe it's just that I've always enjoyed looking down. I don't know how many other people really like to do this. Maybe a lot. My brother is even better at it than I am, but maybe it's just my tiny family.

The second kind of pleasure has to do with pieces fitting together. Whereas the first pleasure was instantaneous, the mind effortlessly constructing the whole beer bottle around the little trapezoid, this pleasure is slightly more patient, involving some actual time and distance. In this second type, as I walk along I notice that some second scrap is the color of something I saw earlier, a ways back, and has a matching edge. The first scrap meant nothing to me, but my brain on its own seems to have believed that one thing may later connect to another thing, and this built-in autonomic faith apparently keeps all the bits animated. Which is to say, the brain anticipates significance; it doesn't know which edge may in fifty yards knit to which other edge, so everything is held, charged with a subliminal glitter along its raw sides.

I like the retroactiveness—or retro-attractiveness—of this process, and I like what it reveals about the mind: that it is cheerfully storing so much all the time, generating infinite cubbies each with its single broken or torn fragment waiting for a match. The whole thing seems so optimistic, as if the mind on its own believes that things are going to fit together.

The pleasures of merely identifying (the piece to the whole) or of merely matching (the piece to a second piece) as one walks along the road can be had without their ever quite reaching the conscious level. Maybe it's like the feeling one would get if she worked out the morning crossword, although I've never done those, just a little sense that it's going to be a good day.

My House

Crispin was ticking like a little Geiger counter as she settled in on a pillow near my head this morning. I was her uranium. But of course with a real Geiger counter, the object isn't just to register the find; somebody has greedy designs on the uranium; somebody wants to get it and sell it. Somebody is getting excited, and the ticking is getting faster and faster.

The marvelous thing about Crispin is that she is not getting excited. She settles down, turns off the tick, and shuts her eyes.

Not everything has to escalate.

I've tried to think about her purr. Why does it always happen at about the same nearness to my head? And why does she purr and then stop purring? What I think is it's a perfect-proximity indicator; it turns on just as she crosses a certain border into perfect proximity, and its only function is to say, You're there. That's why it can quit.

What the cat wants isn't contact but something close to it. Or I could go a little further and blur the border between proximity and contact and say that being almost there (proximity) is the best sort of being there (contact).

Close but no cigar, people say, as though anybody wanted a cigar. Close is much better than a cigar, says Crispin.

This feeling about proximity is related to the exquisite force fields in a house. In the same way that the cat is made perfectly easy (perfectly easy!) by a certain magical relationship between herself and the head of her person, a person is made easy by the magical relationship of various intersecting vectors generated by her chair and table in concert with her lamp, say.

That's how we feel at home, ideally: we feel released to not pay any attention to where we are because we are suspended and weightless in a beautiful web made out of the sweet intersections of the familiar and thoroughly vetted.

A house is a big skull, or at least mine is for me— the container of my brain. Really, I move around in my house disembodied I'm sure.

Or I move around in parts of my house, that is. I wonder if other people are like this and only really use an embarrassingly small amount of their space. If there was an infrared tracker of my movements it would be so irradiated in my bed area that it would burn through the back of Fairfax. There would be serious hatchings in the kitchen and bathroom, lighter arcs out to the mailbox and the driveway for the papers, but the other rooms would be ghostly.

I could apparently sublet much of this lavish thousand-square-foot house.

No: that was a joke. I need all the space I'm not using, just as Crispin needs everything all the way out to the distant perimeter of the fence. She knows if some bad cat has snuck in, and it is very polluting to her rest. We need it empty.

I actually mean empty both physically and mentally.

I have always felt kind of embarrassed that I have to have so much brain I don't use, and even seem to have to aggressively defend the emptiness of. I've never quite come to terms with it because it's so un-American, so inattentive-to-my-bootstraps sounding. It sounds like a character flaw. Dare I say I am in many, many ways *not* curious? That I do not care to add to my mental stores?

Or perhaps I could say, slightly less self-damningly, that though I *am* curious my curiosity is unserious, as if

I am just pretending to be curious about, say, how tall hops plants can grow, because I know that hard little fact is going to drop through my mind just like pretty much everything else. In other words, it is a mind that cannot hold onto a lot but still it is a good mind in its way with long lines of sight unobscured by the heaps of stuff that build up in minds that can build them up.

What my kind of mind likes makes it tick like Crispin's perfect-proximity indicator. My bedroom is full of books and as I pass my eye over them on a given morning, one or another of them is somehow just at the right distance from me, just perfect to open and allow that strange unmaking and remaking of the self, that weird interweaving of brains when things go permeable.

You have to have a lot of extra house around your-self to get this to happen and perhaps it is somehow happening in the extra-house part of the other mind that has become so attractive to me right then. Maybe we share some kind of room for entertaining.

Acknowledgments

Thanks are due to these copyright holders for permission to reprint:

"The Poet Hin," "Dirge," "Autumn," "So to Fatness Come," "Duty was His Lodestar," from *Collected Poems and Drawings* by Stevie Smith reprinted with permission of Faber and Faber Ltd. "Duty was his Lodestar," "So to fatness come," from *All The Poems* by Stevie Smith, copyright © 1937, 1938, 1942, 1950, 1957, 1962, 1966, 1971, 1972 by Stevie Smith. Copyright © 2016 by the Estate of James MacGibbon. Copyright © 2015 by Will May. Reprinted by permission of New Directions Publishing Corp. "Autumn," "Dirge," "The Poet Hin," from *Collected Poems of Stevie Smith* by Stevie Smith, copyright ©1972 by Stevie Smith. Reprinted by permission of New Directions Publishing Corp. "Between Walls," "The Term," from *The Collected Poems: Volume I, 1909-1939* by William Carlos Williams, copyright ©1938 by New Directions Publishing Corp. Reprinted by permission of New Directions Publishing Corp. "Some Simple Measures in the American Idiom and the Varible Foot: Histology" from *The Collected Poems: Volume Ii, 1939-1962,* by William Carlos Williams, copyright ©1962 by William Carlos Williams. Reprinted by permission of New Directions Publishing Corp. "The Paper Nautilus," from *The Collected Poems of Marianne Moore* by Marianne Moore. Copyright © 1941 by Marianne Moore, copyright renewed 1969 by Marianne Moore. Reprinted with the permission of Scribner, a division of Simon & Schuster, Inc. All rights reserved. "Dublinesque," "Forget What Did," "Reference Back," "We Met at the End of the Party," and "Whitsun Weddings" from *The Complete Poems Of Philip Larkin* by Philip Larkin edited by Archie Burnett and "Old Tiger," "The Paper Nautilus," and "The Student" from *New Collected*

Poems by Marianne Moore, edited by Heather Cass White reprinted with permission of Farrar, Straus and Giroux. "We All Know It," "Dear St. Nicklus," and "Reprobate Silver" from *The Poems of Marianne Moore* by Marianne Moore, edited by Grace Schulman, copyright © 2003 by Marianne Craig Moore, Literary Executor of the Estate of Marianne Moore. Used by permission of Viking Books, an imprint of Penguin Publishing Group, a division of Penguin Random House LLC. All rights reserved. "The Effect of Cause Despaired," Something Matters but We Don't," from *Life Supports: New and Collected Poems* by William Bronk reprinted with permission of The Butler Library, Columbia University.